JOBS FOR THE OVER 50s

JOBS FOR THE OVER 50s

How to find work which values your experience

LINDA GREENBURY

PIATKUS

Copyright © 1994 Linda Greenbury

First Published in 1994 by
Judy Piatkus (Publishers) Ltd
5 Windmill Street, London W1P 1HF

The moral right of the author has been asserted

*A catalogue record for this book is available
from the British Library*

ISBN 0-7499-1340-1

Designed by Chris Warner
Typeset by Phoenix Photosetting, Chatham, Kent
Printed and bound in Great Britain by
Mackays of Chatham PLC, Chatham, Kent

For
June Bell
and
Lesley Paiba,
the very best of friends

Acknowledgements

Writers lead a solitary life during the preparation of a manuscript. My thanks go to those special people who have kept me in touch with the real world throughout many months, without whom I should probably have become a vegetable long ago.

I am so grateful to the following for their generous help and information:

B&Q plc
Nigel Corby, CBI/P-E International
Jill Dresden
Jeffrey Ellison, ECCO Age Works
Charlotte Gerlings and Rebecca Gerlings
Alex Lamb MBE, BSc, C Eng, FBIM, Board Appointments and Consultancy Services, Institute of Directors
David Leigh, Prospects Unlimited Management and Training Consultancy
Chris Lucas, Automobile Association
John MacLean Fox, Future Perfect
Gillie McNicol, Animal Aunts
David A. Maxwell BA(Econ) FCA
Angela Milligan, British Executive Service Overseas
Kate Mortimer, Training Division, Age Concern
Sue Shortland, Confederation of British Industries, Employee Relocation Council
Maggie Smith and Lifeskills Communications Ltd, for permission to reproduce the exercise 'What Motivates Me?' from *Branching Out* (2nd edn, 1992, Mercury Books, Gold Arrow Publications Ltd)
Ivor Spencer, Guild of Professional Toastmasters

and everyone else upon whom I have eavesdropped, or have pestered or bored stiff about work opportunities for the over 50s, many of whom were much younger and far wiser than me.

Things need to change in the world around us if we are to make the most of the new possibilities, if we are not to keep on trying to use yesterday's answers to deal with the quite different problems of tomorrow. But we also need to change ourselves.

CHARLES HANDY
The Age of Unreason, 1989

Contents

Introduction

You're writing a – what? A book about work opportunities for whom – the over 50s? You must be joking! Jobs for people over 50 just do not exist. It's OK if you're under 35, but there's nothing for us . . .

So SAID MANY OF THE 50+ JOB SEEKERS I've met during the writing of this book. Yet every employer, institution, book, article or report that I have come across during months of research suggests that there is widespread understanding of the experience and potential of mature adults. What seems to be missing is a change in approach and attitude – not only from organisations and their recruitment executives, but also from the vast reservoir of talented mid-stagers themselves.

Right now, many of the comments appear valid. The world of work today is heavily geared towards the young. Newspapers advertise jobs mainly for those in their 20s and 30s. Occasionally, you may find a situation vacant for an over 40, but it is a rare animal. It has even been suggested that unless you 'make it' in a career before your 35th birthday, you probably will not achieve much. What chance is there, then, for the 50+ worker after a career break, redundancy, early retirement or later retirement, or the late starter, to make life more meaningful?

It is all too easy to take a short-term, pessimistic view of the unemployment statistics and recessionary news. Certainly, many valuable, highly qualified and skilled workers have lost their jobs and are facing an uncertain future, possibly for the first time in their lives. And a glance at the international political and economic scene only makes us more pessimistic and despondent.

1

But stop and think for a minute. Remember all the talk years ago about how information technology would eliminate dreary, repetitive work? Of the disappearance of old, dirty, back-breaking jobs? Of falling mortality rates, of cures for smallpox, tuberculosis and pneumonia? Well, all these predictions came true and our lives are certainly better as a result. But we did not understand, then, just how strong an impact all these changes would make upon the work scene. Now, we realise that there is – as ever – a price to pay in terms of fewer jobs and longer lifespans, and many of us do not like the changes very much.

This book is intended for anyone and everyone of 50 years and more, who wants to take hold of their life at this exciting time of change. I want to boost your morale and encourage you to have a go at finding a new answer to your own situation. To begin with, we shall look backwards at the changes during the past years, but, for the most part, this book will look forward: to the success and fulfilment of a new generation, the people of the Third Age.

THE BACKGROUND STORY

I was the second grandchild on both sides of my family, and have strong recollections of my paternal grandmother and maternal grandfather, the only two grandparents who were alive when I was born. I have a treasured photograph of myself, aged 2 years, sitting with my father's mother, then in her mid 50s, and her mother, my great-grandmother, aged over 70, in a country garden. My grandmother – who was younger then than I am now – wears a hat, flowing dress, sensible shoes. For me, she is typical of her generation.

Born in Stroud, Gloucestershire in 1881, my grandmother was trained for nothing. Probably, she left school at 12, with no qualifications and limited horizons. She did the only thing girls could properly do in those days by marrying young. She had two children before she was 21 and eventually gave birth to five surviving children. She was widowed just after her silver wedding, when her youngest child was only nine. With that child and another daughter still at home, my grandmother went into business with her older sons. By the time I arrived, my father and his brother (the eldest two) were employed elsewhere. The third son, however, maintained her for the rest of her life. She lived long enough to see the arrival of my own first child, her great-granddaughter, but not to know my middle child, a son, born on her birthday.

She would not have thought much about a book like this. To begin with, there would have been few readers as life expectancy was nearly 30 years *less* than we know it today. Then, few people lived to see their 50 birthday, fewer celebrated 60 and a tiny minority went on to more than 70.

In my grandmother's day, the world of work was physically demanding, dirty and endless. One worker in ten was occupied in agriculture, while the rest toiled in factories, mines or domestic service. Childbirth was dangerous, infant mortality uncertain, dirt, disease and danger everyday hazards. For the majority of men, education was minimal and retirement an exception; for the majority of girls, both education and retirement were considered superfluous.

PEOPLE OF THE THIRD AGE

The contrast between my grandmother's day and mine is vivid. When my first grandchild was born, she had all four grandparents and two great-grandmothers alive and well. Everyone was busy: all grandparents worked; one of the 'greats' had her first art exhibition soon after.

A decade or so later, most of us are still at it. My married contemporaries clocked up silver weddings years ago, with ruby celebrations not far away. No one is killing time in a rocking chair: one, a judge, intends to continue until he is 75; another runs his full-time business from home. A third, no longer in professional practice, enjoys several part-time business appointments, in between world-wide travel. Wives and partners work, too, not merely in the traditional, supportive domestic role, but as counsellors, journalists, travel agents and town clerks. Many returned to education in their 40s, taking certificates, diplomas or, like myself, A levels, followed by an Honours degree. My own grandmother would be astonished!

Nowadays, when we attain 20 years of age, we can look forward to an average of 55 more years. In the USA, life expectancy is even higher: beyond 80 years. Demographic developments mean that a quarter of the UK population is presently between 50 and 75 (Carnegie Inquiry, 1993). By the year 2000, the UK Government Actuaries Department estimates that retirees will be 44 per cent of the population. And when the 'baby boomer' generation, the birth explosion following the Second World War, reaches traditional retirement age, the proportion of pensioners will nudge up to 50 per cent. Thus, not only in the UK, but also in the USA and EC, the population will no longer be centred around children or young persons, but will become top heavy – fewer and fewer young workers, and more and more older adults.

When you reach 50, there is a new phase of life about to commence: a fresh start with 15, 20 or more years in prospect, which is as much as infancy, childhood and adolescence put together. With modern medicine and health education, people are sound and active far into their 80s and 90s, with many opportunities for fulfilling and purposeful lives.

My grandmother wears her matronly outfit in my treasured photograph. Now, the only difference between my clothes and those of my grandchildren is that my jeans are bigger than theirs! My Third Age has truly arrived and I hope to share it with you!

WORK OPPORTUNITIES NOW FOR THE OVER 50s

In 1989, the do-it-yourself store B&Q plc opened an over 50s' store in Macclesfield, Cheshire. When they advertised for staff, the response was staggering. B&Q arranged two open days that attracted around 500 people and overall more than 600 applied for 50 available jobs. Nationally, the jobs attracted 7,000 applicants, many of whom had been turned down for jobs elsewhere because of their age. Training, including extra provision for information technology and updated working practices, showed the over 50s to be keen, competent and intensely committed.

The store has been bombarded with praise, boosting customer satisfaction, and reducing staff turnover and absenteeism. The employees, who include 70 year olds, say B&Q has given them a new lease of life and hope for the future, instead of feeling dumped on the scrap heap because of their age. The Macclesfield store has proved to be such a resounding success that the company has doubled its number of employees over 50 to 10 per cent of its 15,000-strong workforce at its 280 stores and has a target of 15 per cent. And it has changed B&Q policy, too: mature applicants are now encouraged to apply for jobs at other stores; employees may continue to work after 60 on a fixed annual contract instead of enforced retirement; and managerial attitudes have become more caring and consultative.

EXPLODING MYTHS AND LEGENDS ABOUT THE OVER 50s

Old age and frailty do not automatically arrive on a certain birthday or with a State pension book. Gerontologists, the medical and scientific experts of old age, suggest that chronological age tells us very little about individual people. As with any other group, older adults vary in biological, psychological and social functioning as much as anyone else. Far more useful is the notion of functional age, the idea that 'we are as old as we feel'. Oldness is very much a state of mind, defined to some extent by society's standards, but also by our own attitudes. Once you believe you are past your best, that is probably how you will appear.

Older does not mean unhealthy. There are undoubtedly more medical problems among 80 year olds than those in their 40s, but with modern drug control and an increasing understanding of healthy living, very few people become incapacitated or severely limited overnight. Incidentally, there is no such disease as 'senility' – for the vast majority, failing intelligence is linked more to the way people are treated rather than to serious illness.

Minds do not suddenly become dull and stupid as they grow older: everyone remains capable of learning throughout their life and there is no age at which this ability ceases. When it looks as if an older adult has failed to grasp something, it is far more likely to be due to fear of making a mistake or because the instructions were unclear. The Open University has illustrated how well old dogs may learn new tricks!

SO, WHY CAN'T I GET A JOB?

Population shifts and inflexible attitudes are only part of the story. During the past few years, there has been a world-wide economic recession resulting in collapsed or reorganised industries. Unofficial forecasts suggest that one out of every two factories in Western Europe will close by the year 2000. Where companies have survived, they have 'unbundled' themselves into smaller business units, merged with similar organisations or gone into partnership to form alliances and networks. The workforce has, therefore, become flattened: in practice, this means fewer people undertaking more jobs.

There have been other vast world-wide shifts, especially within Europe. The collapse of Communism in Eastern Europe has lead to the appearance of new, free market economies and the break-up of huge bureaucracies. For some, this means opportunities; for others it creates instability and uncertainty. The Single European Market has wiped out barriers to the movement of products, goods, services and people. Now, you can go and work anywhere within the Member States, and, just as freely, anyone can seek employment in the UK.

World-wide trade is also in the process of liberalisation as the GATT (General Agreement on Tariffs and Trade) talks progress. Technology is likely to advance even faster than before. Environmental concerns – pollution, waste disposal, the greenhouse effect – are already changing working methods in many industries. New services, such as credit cards and hole-in-the-wall dispensers, have reshaped old occupations. More women are at work than ever before. Cheap labour, especially in the Far East, has forced many clothing and shoe manufacturers overseas.

For many mature job seekers, some familiar jobs have disappeared altogether. Construction, agriculture, manufacturing – all are presently in decline in the UK. In their place come occupations with strange-sounding titles: fibre optics, robotics, bio-engineering.

WHAT ARE THE TRENDS?

All these shifts are resulting in a simple message, as reported in *1990s: Where Will the New Jobs Be?* by Amin Rajan, to whom I am indebted for much of the above information. 'In the current Second Industrial Revolution', he states, 'brain is replacing brawn.'

In the 1990s, Amin Rajan expects fewer full-time jobs, more part-time work, particularly for women, and an increase in self-employment. The notion of multiple careers is increasingly relevant, as individuals make three or four significant career changes during their lives. As well, occupational specialists will become more flexible, as the lines between their jobs and qualifications begin to blur.

I am wary of giving firm predictions about specific jobs or industries where growth is expected. We live in a dynamic world, with an accelerating rate of change. Hence, even the most thoroughly researched studies can only really speculate about the future. At the same time, I realise that an indication of future trends will be helpful to job seekers. With a large pinch of salt and my fingers firmly crossed, here is a selection of services/industries which are expected to grow.

In general:

- anything to do with an older population
- anything to do with business services
- anything to do with career/life planning
- anything to do with childcare for working parents
- anything to do with education
- anything to do with the environment
- anything to do with health, fitness and welfare
- anything to do with personal care
- anything to do with recreation and leisure
- anything to do with security
- anything to do with science and technology

More specifically:

- accountants
- bankers
- beauticians
- career advisers
- chefs
- economists
- financiers
- flight personnel
- hairdressers
- hoteliers
- insurance brokers
- investment advisers
- lawyers
- librarians
- marketing, advertising and public relations
- medical personnel
- pharmacists

- psychologists
- sales staff
- systems analysts
- tax experts
- telecommunication staff
- therapists – physical, occupational etc

Rajan suggests that 'The passport to holding down a job will be through the acquisition of those skills that run with the . . . forces reshaping work'. He looks to the *knowledge workers* of the future, those who are able to adapt, learn, retrain; those with job-specific skills, plus abstract skills such as decision-making, problem-solving and interpersonal communication. Lifetime career planning and continuous learning, both featured in this book, are among his major recommendations.

THE ADVANTAGES OF OLDER WORKERS

There is a growing realisation that the older generation is an undervalued and under-used resource. Their positive and desirable qualities include:

- ability to learn new skills
- commitment to the job
- company loyalty
- enthusiasm
- fewer family distractions
- flexible attitudes
- good attendance records
- high motivation
- fewer romantic preoccupations
- life experience
- lower accident rates
- maturity
- more resistance to job stress
- pride in one's work
- productivity
- proven customer skills
- reduced error rates
- realistic ambitions
- reliability
- self-confidence
- stronger work ethics
- tolerance
- wiser decisions

WHAT DO YOU MEAN BY 'WORK'?

If you were job hunting within the first ten years or so after the Second World War you will probably not remember any particular difficulties in finding a post. Then, the number of situations vacant outstripped the employees available. Youngsters were encouraged to find 'a good steady job' – one with regular promotions and predictable salary increases which would provide them with a living as long as they wished.

For many people, 'work' was – and still remains – 'real work'. 'Real work' means only *paid* employment outside the home, 9–5, five days a week, full time, with take-home pay. It is unrelated to self-employment or freelancing, studying, community or voluntary contributions. It has nothing to do with running a home or bringing up a family, as lots of 'returners' have discovered. Although a woman may have many years of managerial experience in a domestic setting, once she tries to transfer those skills to the workplace, she is thwarted because her 'work' there was unpaid and unrecognised.

But this type of 'real work' is fast disappearing. There is a different, more positive approach to work put forward by Professor Charles Handy in his inspiring vision of tomorrow's world, *The Age of Unreason*. He calls it 'the Work Portfolio'. The Work Portfolio is a multi-pattern of work and a way of describing how the different bits of work in our life fit together to form a balanced whole. It is expected to become the standard way of life for the future and offers a great opportunity for a new range of activities. It is an independent style and attitude which seems to be an ideal basis for people of the Third Age to consider seriously.

There are five main categories of work for the Work Portfolio, some of which I shall be using in the chapters which follow:

- **wage (or salary) work** – money paid to employees for time given;

- **fee work** – money paid to craftspeople, freelancers, and similar, for results delivered;
- **homework** includes all the tasks that go on in the home (cooking, cleaning, children, caring, carpentry, shopping etc.);
- **gift work** is done for free outside the home;
- **study work** – for example, serious training for a sport or learning a new language.

'MAKING LIFE WORK'

'Making Life Work' began in 1984 as a short career/life planning workshop course for women returners. I am not sure where the title originated, but the idea began with my own experience. As a mature student, clutching my new, bright degree certificate, I could not find a job. Employers said 'Well done! Congratulations! But, no – you haven't any experience'. It was not the happiest time of my life, for my children were grown, divorce was looming and the qualification I had worked so hard to achieve seemed to count for nothing.

When I eventually found a job as psychology lecturer in an adult residential college, I began to wonder what happened to other late graduates. I started up college career workshops, based on American guidance methods. Then, suddenly, I found myself out of work again – at 50. The choices were stark: back to square one (clerical work), unemployment or freelancing.

With the advice and support of my son and two very good friends, I set up a specialist career counselling service for women and, at the same time, offered my freshly formatted career workshops to a wider audience. It was warmly received – at adult education colleges, national and local women's groups, foreign service and military wives' associations – and continued until recently when my other freelance and career writing activities took over.

11

WOMEN VERY LATE STARTERS

I obtained my second paid job – the lectureship mentioned above – after a 23-year gap from the workplace. During the gap, I had married, brought up three children, done bits of bookkeeping (mostly unpaid), authored some children's stories, returned to learning and obtained my degree. On paper, my work history was scrappy and muddled. A prospective employer could be more or less guaranteed to take one look at my CV and throw it straight into the rubbish bin. I remember shrieking with delight when the job offer arrived and feeling overjoyed that someone actually wanted me. Mind you, the 'part-time' hours turned out to be something of a myth and the pay was dreadful. I probably could have earned more, in my first probation year, as an office cleaner, but it was all worthwhile in the end. The job changed my life and I shall always feel deeply appreciative of the opportunity.

These days, it is not uncommon for women to find themselves needing a paid job in their middle years. Many have never worked or, if they did, it was – like myself – decades before. The prospect of job-hunting frightens and depresses them. They lack experience, confidence, skills and know-how. The outside world makes it particularly difficult for a woman of 50+: the workplace does not recognise skills acquired in domestic settings, our youthful culture tends to scorn mature appearance while ageism colours all older workers' employment prospects. It is a hard situation to tackle.

The special problem for the older woman who has not worked before or who has stopped work for a number of years is that she often feels she has nothing to show for the years spent in family responsibilities. She believes there is absolutely nothing worthwhile she can earn money for after devoting so many years to housewifery, motherhood, caring. The reality is that she does have work-related personal skills, but in all probability she underestimates them. As Natasha Josefowitz says of women's lives in *Paths to Power*: 'We are already competent administrators, all we need is practice in a new setting. Please don't discount yourself because you have not worked in a job without interruption.'

I cannot emphasise too strongly the need for older women job-seekers to complete a thorough assessment of their skills, strengths and experiences. This book cannot cover all the many detailed steps needed to take you from home into the workplace, but the message contained within the following pages is the same as for any unemployed individual: assess your resources, broaden your horizons and learn the language of self-marketing and job hunting. Make good use of Chapter 2, Consider Yourself, to take stock of your resources; expand choice by consulting Chapters 3, 4 and 5; use Chapter 6, Opening Doors, to review education and training and pay special attention to the over 50s' self-marketing tool kit in Chapter 7. For a selection of more comprehensive self-assessment workbooks, as well as some tips on obtaining expert career help, see Chapter 2.

A wide range of 'women-only' facilities are available, nationwide, if you need further support and help. These are usually 'starter' courses, offering to review life experience, identify transferable skills, and promote confidence and self-esteem, and are valuable stepping stones both for managing a return to work or progressing into further training and education. Some take the form of one-day workshops; there are short (e.g. one term), part-time, evening or Saturday classes; correspondence and distance learning courses. Many have child-care facilities, grants or reduced fees; several contain work-experience modules. The following are useful sources of information:

Women Returners Network, 8 John Adam Street, London WC2N 6EZ publishes *Returning to Work*, an annual directory of UK education and training opportunities (including 'starter' courses, as above) for women. Invaluable comprehensive source of courses and guidance.

Second Chances – Annual Guide to Adult Education and Training Opportunities contains a chapter on women, also one for older people.

Hillcroft College for Women, South Bank, Surbiton, Surrey KT6 6DF offers one-year, part-time and short courses for women without qualifications.

Local adult education colleges Contact your local careers service, Job Centre, reference library, educational guidance for adults service or education department for details of 'New Opportunities for Women (NOW)' or similarly titled courses. The Employment Service provides free services for registered unemployed, although there are restrictions. Enquire for up-to-date provisions.

The Penguin Careers Guide (9th edn) contains a section on late start and return to work; also has 'Late Start' information included for each main career.

The Kogan Page Mature Students Handbook is an annual publication detailing nationwide courses at all levels.

Open University 'Women Into Management' course concentrates on self-awareness and self-confidence with personal exploration exercises and CV help. Contact The Associate Student Central Office, PO Box 76, The Open University, Milton Keynes MK7 6AN.

The Pepperell Unit at the Industrial Society (Robert Hyde House, 48 Bryanston Square, London W1H 7LN) runs short courses, workshops and residential courses.

National Extension College has personal development correspondence courses. NEC, 18 Brooklands Avenue, Cambridge CB2 2HN.

HOW THIS BOOK WILL HELP YOU

This book contains many of the core ingredients from the workshop courses, adapted and augmented for men and women aged 50+. There are many reasons why you may be reading it:

14

perhaps you have been put out of work, left employment by choice, want a career change, are a late starter, look to re-enter the workplace after a gap or need to make the post-employment phase of your life fulfilling and purposeful. Whatever your situation, there is something here for you, to broaden your horizons, and put your talents, interest and potential to good use.

You may feel it is enough to browse through the pages and just think about a few ideas. If you are seriously hunting for wage work, this is insufficient. Re-entering the workplace from any non-employed position is always less than easy. Employers are wary, applicants anxious. Career gaps (for whatever reason) tend to sap one's confidence and self-esteem, evaporate skills, increase stress. You are strongly advised to work through *all* the early chapters in order to gain knowledge and information about how others can help you and how you can help yourself.

Chapter 1 looks at coping with change, including pre-retirement planning, practical steps for organising the early days without work, how to manage your time, how best to take care of yourself, keeping your spirits up, how to stop forgetting, long-term unemployment, people and places for support, and a short overview of the financial implications of paid work on a pension.

Chapter 2 is the all-important self-assessment chapter. Do not miss this career/life planning overview, whether or not you want full-time work, as it will assist you to gain new insights and create a more personally meaningful life. You will also find a section on career counselling in this chapter.

Chapter 3 contains details of wage work, while fee and gift work are dealt with in Chapter 4, with freelancing and self-employment tackled in Chapter 5. The all-important 'continuous learning' information may be found in Chapter 6.

Chapter 7 deals with personal marketing for older adults, seeking work perhaps for the first time for many years. Chapter 8 looks at current technology, settling in, your next job and asks 'Are you indispensable?' In Chapter 9 we look at relocation, moving abroad, what over 50s can do now, Grey Power resources and a vision of the future.

At the back of this book, you will find a selection of outline

CVs to adapt for your personal circumstances; a bibliography; and a list of useful addresses.

FINALLY . . .

If your past work portfolio had only one item in it and that was your job or career, or bringing up children, and you believe the only way forward is to have more of the same, then you are limiting yourself. Whatever your reason for seeking a new direction, re-entering the workplace, changing course or switching lifestyle, the first, most important step you can take is to reconsider your options and broaden your horizons. If you are willing, the following chapters can start helping you – now.

So, are there work opportunities for the over 50s? The answer is, YES! Wage work, fee work, home work, gift work, study work – there is plenty to choose from in the following pages for both men and women.

1

Your Life in Your Hands

COPING WITH CHANGE

BY THE TIME WE REACH OUR HALF CENTURY, most of us have undergone many changes in our lives: from schoolchild to worker, from bachelor/spinsterhood to partnership, from partner to parent. And, as we learn of each day's news, we are aware how the events around us impact on our lives at an ever-increasing pace.

We learn to cope with change. If the change is pleasant and expected, we look forward to the coming event and our excitement is a *positive* stress. For example, when a new baby is on the way, there are nine long months to learn (a little!) about parent craft, prepare a nursery, attend ante-natal classes, choose names and dream about holding a child in our arms. We know, in advance, we are about to change role and status. If, on the other hand, something goes sadly adrift during the pregnancy, an unanticipated and unpleasant event, we seldom expect the intense feelings of disappointment, bereavement and loss which follow. This *negative* stress and strain may be overwhelming.

Psychologists Holmes and Rahe developed a social readjustment rating scale (1967) with which to measure important life changes. They found redundancy and retirement, two major life events, to be among the top ten most stressful changes

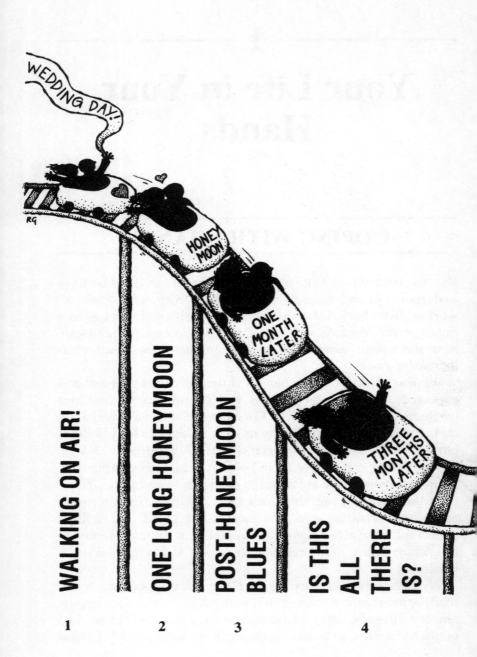

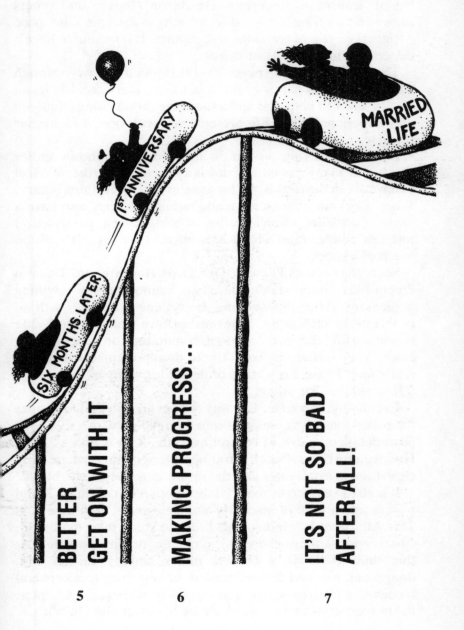

5   6   7

(marriage scores higher). From this work, a general understanding of 'transitions' emerged. Dr Barrie Hopson and others showed how a transition – a discontinuity in a person's life space – triggers a cycle of reactions and feelings. It is helpful to have a closer look at this cycle of stages.

The Roller-Coaster (pages 18–19) shows a journey through what should be a happy event in our lives, marriage, but it can also be used to help you understand the mood swings that you may experience when life presents you with one of its nastier surprises.

Phase 1, Walking on Air, is a feeling of euphoria and/or shock. For many, a wedding day is a dream come true. We feel as if we are in the clouds; nothing seems real, everything is hazy. When a person is suddenly made redundant, they also have a sense of disbelief, often a feeling of being frozen, paralysed. 'I just can't understand what's happened,' they say. 'It's all too much of a shock.'

Soon after comes Phase 2, One Long Honeymoon. This is a dream-like numb state where we cannot accept anything unpleasant. After the wedding, everything is blissful, with no problems, no difficulties. New retirees have 'honeymoons' – life is wonderful, they say, without commuting or watching the clock. They ignore any boredom or disappointments they may really feel. Phase 2 is a stage of denial for many individuals or false optimism for others.

Eventually, of course, actuality catches up with us. Down goes the roller-coaster, zooming us into depression, with a feeling of powerlessness, a loss of control over life. This is Phase 3, The Honeymoon Blues. It is a frustrating and angry stage, where early cheerfulness evaporates and the future looks decidedly bleak.

It is all too easy to become fatalistic as a result of Phase 3, and to sink into a state of inactivity and listlessness. At Phase 4, Is This All There Is?, individuals begin to study their lives more closely and ask themselves, 'Is this the reality of my new life?' At this time there is a choice: either sinking further into disappointment and disillusionment; or beginning to accept and recognise a fresh existence. For those who do begin to accept it, the move carries them towards Phase 5, Better Get On With it.

Soon, activity and energy help you along to Making Progress, Phase 6. You are feeling better now and understanding more about the meaning of the event which has changed your world. And once you grasp this understanding firmly, your morale improves and you become accustomed to your new way of life. All this brings you a sense of balance, everyday calm and through the process of change: Phase 7, Married Life – It's Not So Bad After All!

PLANNING FOR CHANGE

Next, you need to know about pre-retirement planning; practical steps for organising the early days without work; job clubs and self-help groups; how to manage your time; how best to take care of yourself; how to stop becoming forgetful; keeping up your spirits; about long-term unemployment; about the people and places who may be able to support you during this time of change; plus you need an overview of the financial implications of paid work if you are on a pension. The rest of this chapter is devoted to these topics.

Pre-retirement planning

Many organisations provide pre-retirement courses for their employees. Individuals should take up all these opportunities, not just to sort out their finances – pension planning, for example, may require several years to put into operation – but also to begin to think through what they want to do with their lives.

Research by Future Perfect, a commercial pre-retirement organisation, suggests that people may delay planning the transition to retirement, refusing to believe that it is really going to happen to them. They tend to be unaware of the real implications of this vulnerable stage until it affects them personally. Once the leaving date looms, though, the reality hits them hard and they panic – Phase 2 of Coping With Change. Instead, they should start to focus well in advance, not only on the mechanics of budgeting on a pension but, more important, on discovering a purpose in life, and an independent attitude towards life and work.

Pre-retirement planning courses are available to everyone, not just employees. Independent organisations and employer-sponsored courses usually contain several core topics, such as finance, health activity, leisure, housing and lifestyle adjustment. Participants' partners/spouses may also attend.

The Pre-Retirement Association (PRA) of Great Britain and Northern Ireland, a national charity set up in 1964, is the national body for retirement counselling. Their Retirement Preparation Service is available to companies and individuals. The PRA also publishes an annual *Directory of Pre-Retirement Courses*, available from PRA, Nodus Centre, University Campus, Guildford, Surrey GU2 5RX. They also produce a cassette tape called *Talking Retirement*.

Useful information

Future Perfect, 6 Langley Street, London WC2H 9JT: 'Third Age Transition' Workshops, follow-through sessions and support for individuals and companies.

Greater London Association for Pre-Retirement, Seacoal House, 9 Seacoal Lane, London EC4M 7HY.

Insurance companies, such as Prudential and Standard Life, offer pre-retirement seminars.

Jewish Care, Training Department, 221 Golders Green Road, London NW11 9DQ (workshops).

Millstream Pre-Retirement Ltd, Mill House, South Harting, Petersfield, Hampshire GU31 5LF (senior executives).

Open University, PO Box 188, Milton Keynes MK7 6DH: study pack 'Planning Retirement'.

Prime Time Retirement Services, 63 Lincoln's Inn Fields, London WC2 3JX (financial planning, lifestyle adjustment, women only courses from 40+).

Retirement Counselling Service, Turret House, The Avenue, Amersham, Bucks HP7 0AB (courses).

Retirement Education Centre, Bedford College, 6 Rothsay Gardens, Bedford MK40 3QB.

Scottish Pre-Retirement Council, Alexandra House, 204 Bath Street, Glasgow G2 4HL.

Practical steps for organising the early days without work

Preliminaries

Experts suggest that it is a mistake to take a long holiday or 'relax' for months following redundancy or retirement. The problem is that once you have slackened and relaxed, you may have a problem revving up and getting started again. Then your mind refuses to focus on what you want to do next or how to set about it.

Stop procrastinating; instead ask yourself how you are going to get your act together. A daily task list is a useful notion. Make a list of everything you want to achieve during the day, including letters, telephone calls, visits, research. As you complete each task, reward yourself by firmly crossing out the item on your list. Carry over any unfinished jobs to the following day's list.

Work opportunities will not appear by magic without you taking action. Begin by finding out what job-seeking facilities exist locally.

Have you been to the local Job Centre and Job Club (see next section)? Have you checked through the telephone directory, *Yellow Pages* and *Thomson's Guide* for relevant employment agencies? Have you visited the library (reference section), and looked up appropriate trade and professional associations who may have appointments registers? Have you read the local and national newspapers, trade journals and specialist magazines to update your knowledge and scan vacancies? If not, *do it now*!

The importance of a routine

You must keep up a regular, Monday-to-Friday weekday routine. Get up in the morning at the same time as you would if you were going to work. Eat sensibly. Dress in businesslike clothes, even if you are just going to the library. Leave home at a reasonable time, complete with briefcase and umbrella. Walk briskly at least twice a day. Keep lunch/snacks nourishing, light and inexpensive – an apple is better than fast food, a wholemeal sandwich better than salty crisps. Eat slowly. Put in a reduced but worthwhile work day towards your job search: six hours is probably about right. Make the evenings and weekends different – continue to enjoy the family, spend time with your partner, keep in touch with friends, hobbies, interests and sports.

Job Clubs and self-help groups

A system of Job Clubs for the unemployed (not executives) has been set up by the Department of Employment for those who have been out of work for more than six months and who are in receipt of benefit. They will pay your fares to attend, and offer free advice and support. They also provide use of typewriters, photocopiers, stamps, stationery, newspapers and business directories. Ask at your Job Centre for details.

Executives have access to resources such as the Institute of Directors, Institute of Personnel Management, headhunters and outplacement consultants (for more information on Outplacement, see page 34, below).

Self-help groups are often started up by someone who is retired or redundant themselves. Projects like this usually include networking and publicity as a means of attracting jobs, plus many of the Job Club facilities. The support of others in the same situation can be encouraging and boost your confidence, providing they do not descend into 'groan groups'. Enquire locally for groups in your area.

The Trades Union Congress (TUC) (23–28 Great Russell Street, London WC1B 3LS) runs a national network of Centres for the Unemployed as do a wide range of organisations including churches and synagogues. Ask at your local library, Citizens Advice Bureau, Unemployed or Welfare Rights Centre, or Technical and Enterprise Council (TEC).

Managing your time

When I was first on my own after a long period as a very busy wife and mother, I found myself floundering. I had no job and I was so accustomed to pacing myself to the family routine, that, when the family no longer existed, I scarcely knew which day of the week was which, what to do or when. Eventually, my elder daughter sat me down and gave me a good talking to. 'Mum,' she said, 'you have to make the weekends different from the weekdays and mornings different from the afternoons. You can't go on like this.' She was right: my so-called freedom had turned into a trap.

I was not alone. Unemployment, whether it is from paid or unpaid work, is perhaps the only time an adult has unstructured time available. As a schoolchild, teenager, worker and homemaker, your hours and days were governed and controlled by outside demands. When you have no work to do, you may have all the time in the world but lack the experience to know what to do with it. Soon you could find the days getting longer and duller. As author Eldwood N. Chapman says in *Comfort Zones*, retirement is '. . . a kind of no-man's-land. There are few reference points; everything must come from within. You must decide on your own . . . there are few guideposts'.

If we are not very careful, time slips away without our really noticing. How often have you said: 'I don't know where all the time has gone'? As a 50 year old, already you will have spent 438,000 hours sleeping, learning, working, looking after yourself and family. The future time available to you may be half as much again – or many hours more . . . how do *you* want to spend your life? Use the following exercise to help you organise your time constructively.

EXERCISE 1.1

The Time Exercise

Instead of the old adage about 'making your bed and lying on it', take a look at the two time trifles shown here. Time trifle A shows how many of us spend our working lives. You will see that we spend around half of our time in work. Home life — domestic responsibilities and maintenance, child and elder care, etc. — and leisure — watching TV, socialising, cultural activities, sports — occupy the remainder. (Travel, personal care, etc. may either be sectioned separately or included in the work category). That tiny little swirl on the top of the trifle is our leisure time — a kind of decorative extra that we allow ourselves during our most active days.

Time trifle B shows an entirely different story: here we have lots of leisure and plenty of home life. This illustration could, perhaps, represent the way time is spent by those who do not wish or are unable to work.

Individuals vary in their daily routine and time needs, so you should now draw two diagrams of your own. The first should reflect your past activities, while the second will represent how, ideally, you would like to spend your time now.

If you have clear ideas of your own about the way you wish to live, you will have little difficulty (but a lot of fun!) creating your illustration. If you are stuck for ideas, think about these possibilities:

- full-time work either as an employee or in your own business, much the same as previously;
- part-time, contract or temporary paid work, plus non-paid work, more leisure and some second chance education;
- leisure mainly, plus volunteer work and optional odd jobs (paid or free).

When drawing up your time trifle give plenty of thought to the proportions of the trifle you wish to allow for each segment of your life.

How to take care of yourself

Physical health

Any job seeker who is over 50 must make a trip to the doctor for a complete physical check-up. Prospective employers will be asking themselves (and you, probably, as well) questions such as 'Is this person fit and healthy? How much time will be needed for sick leave? Can this worker stand the pace?' You can forestall these and similar questions by getting in shape, and presenting an active and energetic image.

Your general practitioner may provide a 'lifestyle' check-up, but should this not be available, consider investing in a private consultation or attending a specialist medical centre. BUPA, PPP and similar associations offer private health screening consultations for men and women all over the UK. Additionally, have your eyes tested and obtain new spectacles if necessary; your teeth, feet and hearing should also be thoroughly checked.

Physical exercise

Follow medical advice to reduce blood pressure, weight, smoking and alcohol consumption. Keep an eye on your diet: a trim, youthful and well-kept body enhances your job prospects. Take up walking, swimming, dancing, cycling, table tennis, keep-fit, golf, bowling – any sport or activity which is gentle and safe and approved by your medical adviser. Classes for over 50s are available in most sports and leisure centres, usually with concessions for those over State retirement age. Join a club, circle, group, course for support and encouragement; try yoga or T'ai-chi Chu'an for stimulating but gentle alternatives to traditional exercise.

Mental activity

Mental exercise is just as important as physical fitness. Crosswords, bridge, Scrabble™, jigsaws, chess, logic puzzles, acrostics, quizzes – these and similar indoor games help stretch and maintain alertness. Many 'mind' games are solo activities, which is fine up to a point, but too much time alone may create difficulties. Try to involve yourself with other people whenever you can, even if it is just a fellow crossword addict at the end of the telephone! Bridge and Scrabble™ groups abound; other clubs may be available locally such as family and local history projects, writers' groups, amateur dramatics, choral groups, musical gatherings. Enquire at your public library for details and consult your nearest adult education college.

Consider taking a short course at one of the many adult residential colleges or summer schools, thus combining a holiday, new friends and an interest. Some summer schools (Millfield and Taunton, for example) offer activities for all age groups, so why not make it a family holiday or take a favourite youngster along with you as a treat? For more on this see Chapter 6.

Forgetfulness

Older adults frequently worry about their memory. They say they 'can't remember things so well now' or that they can remember events from a long time ago, but not more recent happenings.

The first point to make is that no one remembers everything. Throughout our lives, we select what we want to store in our memory, and develop effective methods to search and come up with the piece of information we need. Later on, however, the shape of memory, and our storage and retrieval system seems to change. A word, a name or a fact just will not come to mind when you want it. Events from 40 years ago are quite clear, but when you are asked what you did last week, you just cannot remember. If you have always had a 'good' memory, it is very frustrating and not a little frightening.

Current research suggests some loss of memory in older adults is normal – it happens to everyone. But this does not mean it is unavoidable or that there is nothing you can do about it. In fact, it is only a particular aspect of memory which seems to be affected. As far as we know at present, we have several different memory systems which link together. Long-term memory seems to remain unimpaired as we age, so we do not forget our childhood experiences, how to ride a bicycle or what cheese tastes like. The system that does appear to change is our working or short-term memory, a temporary storage bank which we need for short periods of time. Between the two, it is thought we have some kind of brain workings which transfer experiences from one system to another and makes them stick.

EXERCISE 1.2

Memory joggers

If you want to prevent memory loss, try these exercises.

- **Repetition** Americans have the recall of names down to a fine art! When they meet you for the first time, they will keep on repeating your name over and over again. It is not just politeness – repetition really helps the memory process. Try it yourself next time you meet someone new or want to remember a telephone number: repeat the information frequently for the first five minutes, then at lengthening intervals during the day to 'top up' the storage process. If you get it wrong, start again. If you are returning to learning or settling in with new work colleagues, this exercise is really useful.

- **Concentrate** Pay attention to what is being said or demonstrated (additional reasons to check your eyes and hearing). New learning will become properly incorporated into your data bank if you concentrate hard.

- **Relax** Anxiety reduces our attention span and interferes with the memory process.

- **Imagery** A good way to remember things is to link them to a picture in your mind. Her name is Jenny? Think of a wren. The more bizarre and vivid the image, the better it works.

- **Association** Associating a piece of new information to something already stored can be very useful. Try linking numbers together in pairs or adding them up, for example a telephone number may be made up entirely of odd or even numbers, or come to a total which is the same as your date of birth or a famous date such as 1066!

- **Make lists** of things to do and tick them off when they are accomplished.

- **Keep a diary** of what you want to do or have done. It need not be a literary masterpiece, merely a memory jogger.

- **Be organised** Put keys, money, credit cards, important objects and papers in the same place every time. If a change is necessary (if you move, for example), write down some clues to your new hidey-holes. I once spent several months hunting for a particular piece of jewellery. Before going on holiday, I hid it so carefully that not only could a thief not find it, neither could I! It turned up eventually, but not before my blood pressure and embarrassment had risen to unprecedented heights.

- **Mnemonics** These are jingles or rhyming key words which you link to the items to be remembered by creating absurd, sexual or colourful pictures in your mind. More details can be found in Tony Buzan's book *Use Your Head* (BBC Books).

- **Keep a keen mind!** If you put any kind of machine into cold storage for 30 or 40 years, it is bound to become rusty and perform poorly. Keep your brain machine exercised, curious, fit, enthusiastic and busy.

Keeping up your spirits

Don't let yourself go

- **Men:** keep your hair trimmed, shirts clean, suits pressed, your shoes repaired and polished.

- **Women:** invest in an easy, up-to-date hairstyle; wear tasteful, muted colours; and keep shorts, sandals and midriffs for the beach.

- **Both:** spend time on general grooming. Don't waste interview opportunities with grubby nails or a lack of personal freshness. Stand up straight, keep your head up and look people in the eye!

Don't be afraid to ask for help

It is not an admission of failure, nor is it a crime, to admit you are out of work. You are not guilty of idleness or laziness when a company closes its plant and you become jobless. If family or friends are embarrassed by your non-employment, do not burden them with your problems. Instead, find others to support you: those who have been in a similar position in the past; employee assistance resources from your previous employer; professional counselling services; your doctor or place of worship. Avoid using alcohol or similar as a crutch – it will drain your finances, health and prospects.

Long-term unemployment

If you have been out of work for more than a year, you are not alone: most research suggests that this applies to 50 per cent of unemployed people. But it does not mean you should be idly twiddling your thumbs. If you look again at Professor Handy's concept of the Work Portfolio, on page 10, you will see there are many different options open to you to keep you focused and in touch with the workplace. You will, of course, have your 'off' days – everyone does, but you will avoid falling into the deep, fatalistic despair described in Phase 4 of the Roller-Coaster. Remember, when jobs are short, it does not mean no one will ever work again; instead, it means it will just take longer.

There is no one answer which will be of use for everyone in this situation, but the experience of re-entry women may be helpful. They well understand how easy it is to become an unsaleable commodity in the job market. Family and domestic responsibilities frequently result in a person becoming invisible and devalued in the paid workplace. Returners are making use of the numerous education and training opportunities as a bridge into jobs. They are prepared to take a step down in their employment level, even if they are over-qualified, in order to get a toehold on the workplace ladder, and they have come to understand that promotion and career upward mobility is their responsibility, not that of their employer. The Women Returners Network has achieved considerable progress on their behalf and may well be a model which other groups of out of work people could emulate.

If your job hunt has been unsuccessful and you feel discouraged, it is all too easy to blame everyone and everything else for your condition. But, before you challenge world-wide economic policies, or blame the weather or the new technology, ask yourself a few questions.

Have you set yourself too narrow a range of job opportunities? If your previous work has disappeared or become obsolete, you must review your transferable skills and look at new fields. Unlike those who object to motorways and dream about a car-free world and a return to horse-drawn traffic, you must be realistic and deal with what is currently available.

Are you too embarrassed, shocked or shy to ask for help? It is all too easy to understand how difficult it may be to approach friends, contacts, advice centres and Job Clubs, especially after you have always held down a good job and perceive yourself as a hard, loyal worker. It is often just too hard to accept yourself as 'unemployed'; on the dole or as a menial worker. Instead, you may have been sitting at home waiting for the telephone to ring, answering newspaper advertisements or even pretending to go to work every day without actually doing so. If this is you, please rethink your situation – now. You have not committed a capital offence by being middle-staged and out of work; in fact, you are probably one of the majority these days. Take hold of that initiative you were once so proud of and go out to contact someone to help you.

Support from people and places

Outplacement services

Outplacement counselling is sometimes provided by an employer as part of a separation package. If you are still employed (but about not to be) and your employer does not provide this service, ask for it or the money to buy it. The range of possible services is very large: some offer full career counselling, job search support, personal marketing, aid with CVs, networking, office facilities, advice on compensation packages, interview techniques and follow-up advice. Others give a basic CV service, or just one seminar and a chat. Costs vary from £50 to many hundreds – or even thousands – of pounds.

Before signing up for anything, obtain details from several consultancies, and try to decide what you need and expect from the service. Do not rush. Avoid any 'career evaluation' which may be linked to sales promotions or similar. Take advantage of any free initial interview offers. Aim to work with a counsellor of a similar age, stage and background to yourself, and with whom you feel comfortable and confident.

On the plus side, outplacement counselling offers a chance to indulge yourself, talk about any and everything you have ever wanted to do or be, and test out your ideas, however fanciful. Individual coaching for interviews with video feedback is invaluable. However much you may cringe at the thought, it is better to make a fool of yourself in a practice run than the real thing! Counsellors may advise and assist you with many tips, contracts and job leads. You may also be offered other facilities: office space, telephones, photocopying and/or secretarial help.

Remember, though, that outplacement counsellors are business people. They should not attempt to 'guarantee' results, pressure you into expensive programmes of help or unrealistically build up your hopes. Always check that the organisation abides by the Institute of Personnel Management's (IPM) code of conduct for outplacement providers, and are members either of the IPM, the British Psychological Society or British Association for Counselling, and, if involved in psychological assessment, that they have a recognised Statement of Competence in Occupational Testing.

For details of career counselling, see Chapter 2.

Partners/spouses

I met an early retired accountant recently and asked him how life was going. Unbeknown to me, his wife was standing nearby, 'Don't bother to ask him,' she interposed. 'It's me you need to talk to.'

She went on: 'After all those years of bringing up children and looking after Mother, I'd just about got my life sorted out. A part-time job at the CAB, voluntary work with the church, time for the garden and the grandchildren – and even a few hours to myself at long last. Suddenly, there he is, hanging around all day long wanting to know what I am doing every few minutes, complaining if I come home two minutes late from a meeting and telling me to retire too. I can't go anywhere by myself these days. He has to drive me everywhere and keeps on about 'my' car being such an extravagance now. And as for meals – well, I haven't cooked so many meals for years. Now its food, food, food all day long. It's just like having a toddler around again.'

Mid-stagers are often surprised when their partners are not thrilled to have them around the home all and every day. Ask yourself: what is the longest period of time you have ever spent together up to now? My guess it that your answer will be perhaps two, maybe three, weeks at most . . . and that was probably on holiday. Now, perhaps at a time when there are worries and tensions about the future, both of you are thrust together under the same roof almost all the time.

If you are the newly-at-home partner, tread very carefully indeed during the early days. Your everyday presence is most likely to feel like an invasion of territory and a loss of privacy. If you start behaving like a schoolchild, hanging around the home, demanding attention but never offering to help, your relationship is very likely to suffer. Spend time on your own, go out of the house regularly, respect each other's routines, and allow your partner time and space on their own.

Partners/spouses can offer greater support if they understand the culture shock and sense of loss the newly-at-home is experiencing. Take another look at the Roller-Coaster on pages 18–19 in Chapter 1 and consider where your homebird is on the ride. If they are at an early stage of transition, recognise that the euphoria and optimism will not last, and be ready to offer sympathy and empathy but never pity. Try not to take their distress personally and give them time for adjustment. The household routine may be a lifeline to someone whose everyday structure has collapsed. So, keep up your own routine – in and out of the house – as much as possible, for their sake as much as your own.

Later, you may well become the scapegoat for all that is wrong and disappointing; you may have to find more work yourself and become the main breadwinner. Controlling your own anger and resentment is not easy when everything is in a state of upheaval and what was once a tower of strength sags into gloom.

Make sure you have trustworthy others with whom to share your feelings or seek counselling help yourself to ease the burden. You will understand, too, that a time could arise when your partner's dejection requires professional assistance. Make contact with medical advisers if you are worried about yourself or others.

You certainly cannot be expected to cope with everything without complaint. Yes, you must prepare to take on a stronger role than before; yes, you can encourage and assist with ideas, diet, exercise; yes, you can take a job of your own and make a contribution . . . but, no – you cannot and should not become therapist, servant or nanny. The very best help a partner or spouse can offer the newly-at-home is to help them help themselves.

Single and unattached?

The greatest problem for the non-employed, unattached single person is isolation. Whether you are happy or miserable at redundancy or retirement, it is all too easy to become bored, neglectful and lack motivation when you are at home alone 24 hours a day. Work provides social contact as well as income; living by yourself with little interaction with others means shrinking horizons and insufficient stimulation.

'I can't be bothered . . .' is a danger signal! Take action to meet new people and cherish old friendships. Use the tips above to organise your time and activities while caring for yourself adequately. Eat proper meals, take some exercise, keep fit. There is nothing wrong with TV in moderation, but it is as much 'chewing gum for the mind' for older adults as it is for youngsters. Get out and about! Join a group, a Job Club, an activity class, a study set and involve yourself with others. Think about voluntary work, too, at least in the short term.

Should you find yourself becoming low and feeling depressed, do not hesitate to obtain help. Relatives may be able to help on an informal basis, as may past professional, educational or trade associates. If the condition lasts for longer than a few days, you should consult your doctor. Your priest, minister or rabbi may be able to help (some religious organisations provide counselling, job clubs and voluntary opportunities). In an emergency, the Samaritans (under 'S' in the phone book) will talk and listen any time of the day or night, every day of the year.

Financial implications of paid work if you are on a pension

Finance is a very large subject, far too big to detail in one book. Nevertheless, there are several aspects of finance related to paid work if you are on a pension that you should know about. An overview is provided below, but you should take note that any information offered is constantly subject to change. Always obtain expert up-to-date advice.

Taxation

Taxation does not disappear if you are retired. Normally all your income is assessable for tax purposes. This means earnings from work including bonuses, commissions and fees, State and occupational pensions, and most investment income. Everyone is entitled to a tax-free personal allowance, which is increased at 65 and then again at 75. But, if your total income exceeds a certain limit, the higher allowance will be reduced.

Inform your local tax office if you take paid work. The responsibility to do so is on you, not your employer. Your tax office, or your last employer's tax office, are the places to go if you are unsure of anything to do with your tax position. Look in the phone book under 'Inland Revenue – Taxes, HM Inspectors of'.

Other help and advice on taxation is obtainable from your local Citizens' Advice Bureau, Age Concern or your accountant.

National Insurance

You are required to pay National Insurance contributions up to statutory retirement age. Under that age, it all depends how much you earn, with the amount payable varying from year to year depending on the Budget and current Finance Act. If you are over State retirement age, obtain an exemption card (Form CF384 Certificate of Exemption) to give to your employer. Contributions are required from self-employed and freelance workers. For up-to-the-minute information, contact your local Department of Social Security for relevant leaflets.

Pensions

Joining a new occupational pension in middle age may be complicated, so think very carefully before considering early retirement. Recent legislation allows employers to pay a full pension, without any deductions, at any age between 50 and 70, provided the employee has been with the company for at least 20 years. But this is not obligatory. An employer may indeed reduce a retiree's pension and can remain within the law, always assuming there is no change in the present position. If you leave a pension scheme after as little as two years in the company, you may be able to have a refund of your contributions. Ask lots of questions before accepting anything. For further advice, contact the Society of Pension Consultants, Ludgate House, Ludgate Circus, London EC4A 2AB or Occupational Pensions Advisory Service (OPAS), 11 Belgrave Road, London SW1V 1RB.

Good Retirement Guide by Rosemary Brown (1992, Kogan Page) contains useful chapters on money and finances, including detailed information on pensions and tax.

2

Consider Yourself

EXPERTS IN THE CAREERS BUSINESS believe you cannot make worthwhile decisions about your future until you have taken stock of your personal and working past. Professionals use a wide range of questionnaires and objective tests to assess clients, many of which can only be used by qualified psychologists. But you can start on the assessment process by yourself without delay by completing the simple exercises on the following pages.

Self-assessment is important and valuable in its own right, so relax! It is fun, enjoyable, beneficial – and completely confidential. No one else is going to mark or judge you; there is no 'pass' or 'fail'; no 'right' or 'wrong', 'good' or 'bad' answers. All you need is paper and pencil, an uninterrupted hour or two and plenty of honest thought.

Taking the time to think about yourself in a structured way offers many benefits including:

- an overview of what is important to you now
- better information upon which to make decisions
- knowledge about your strengths
- reliable facts for CV preparation
- an appraisal of your skill gaps
- positive material for answering interview questions
- a reminder of forgotten goals, hopes and dreams
- time for yourself, often long lost with work and family life
- a chance to gain increased self-confidence and new insights

It may be tempting to skip the rest of this chapter – please don't! Even if you are currently unemployed, facing a heap of unpaid

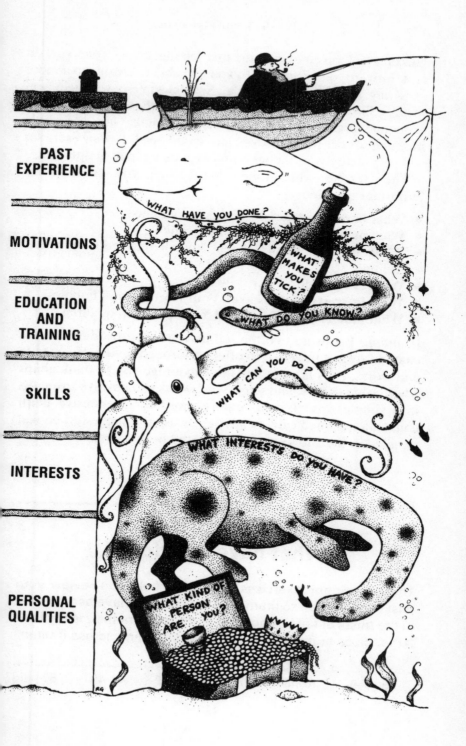

PAST
EXPERIENCE

WHAT HAVE YOU DONE?

MOTIVATIONS

WHAT MAKES YOU TICK?

EDUCATION
AND
TRAINING

WHAT DO YOU KNOW?

WHAT CAN YOU DO?

SKILLS

WHAT INTERESTS DO YOU HAVE?

INTERESTS

PERSONAL
QUALITIES

WHAT KIND OF PERSON ARE YOU?

bills and feel forced to grab the first job that comes your way, do look forward to the time when you feel able to change to a more satisfying and fulfilling lifestyle. Self-assessment will help you identify those choices for a later date. For those of you without economic pressure, wondering how to make life personally meaningful once full-time work has ceased, the following exercises will help clarify your thoughts and explore a range of options.

The exercises which follow aim to help you answer these important questions.

- **What have you done?** Your past experience.
- **What makes you tick?** Your motivations.
- **What do you know?** Your knowledge, education and training.
- **What can you do?** Your skills.
- **What interests do you have?** Your interests and hobbies.
- **What kind of person are you?** Your personal qualities.

(*Caution:* Be aware that the self-assessment procedures in this chapter are not intended to offer a thorough review of your life and work. They are designed to encourage you to think about where you are now, and select your assets and positive strengths in a simple way. If you require more comprehensive help, consult a qualified careers adviser or use the suggested books, detailed in the Bibliography at the end of this book.)

EXERCISE 2.1

What have you done?

There are many exercises devised to help you review your past experiences, so many that their origins have become lost in the mists of time. A popular and simple method is to take a large, piece of paper and draw a straight line across it thus:

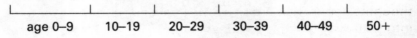

age 0–9   10–19   20–29   30–39   40–49   50+

The left hand marker is your birth and each decade of your life is indicated by the dividing upright line. Make a mark along the line (extend it whenever necessary) to represent where you are now in your life. Now, show the turning points in your life in each decade with symbols or different colours to indicate what you have done.

You may find it easier to set down several lines, thus:

Age 0–9

Age 10–19

Age 20–29

Age 30–39

Age 40–49

Age 50+

Use the arrangement that you find most helpful. Show all your experiences: your education, training, jobs, relationships, hobbies and family events. Mark the pleasant events as well as the less enjoyable. Jot down your age at the time of each event.

Make a note of what you achieved during and as a result of that experience – dates, names and addresses of employers; why an event became special or exceptional to you. Continue placing as many marks as you can on your diagram to capture the major experiences of your life.

Reflect now on the following questions and jot down a few thoughts about each one. You may gain some useful insights into your way of coping with change.

1. Is there a pattern in your experiences: are they happy, painful, voluntary, imposed upon you, planned, unanticipated?

2. What have you learned from these experiences?
   — When a sudden, unexpected event occurred, how did you manage to cope?
   — When an anticipated event occurred, how did you prepare for the change?

3. Make a list of your important life experiences.

4. Project your line forward in time. What would you like to experience? What dreams do you have? How can you make these things happen?

YOUR MOTIVATION

For many people, money, status symbols and financial security are good enough rewards from a job. Others prefer to help the unfortunate, fulfil their creativity, acquire power, authority, recognition and independence. These are *motivations*, those needs and energies which propel us towards a lifestyle, fulfilling our dreams and gaining us satisfaction in life.

Mid-life is an excellent stage at which to explore what motivates you and discover what you want in the future. The following exercise is from Maggie Smith's book, *Changing Course*, based on her programmes in career transitions and mid-life planning with individuals and organisations.

Follow the instructions as directed. When complete, analyse your lists – there may be gaps in column 3 – How Can I Find Them In Future? You will be able to return to this column as you progress through the rest of this chapter.

EXERCISE 2.2

What makes you tick?

WHAT MOTIVATES ME? WHAT DO I WANT IN THE FUTURE?

What to do: Tick in column 1 those factors which apply to you. Then tick column 2 for those you want to keep. There will probably be some blanks in column 3 which you can fill in as you complete more exercises.

FACTORS IN JOB	FACTORS IN MY PRESENT JOB	I WANT TO KEEP (OR TO INCLUDE)	HOW CAN I FIND THEM IN FUTURE?
Accommodation (living in)			
Applause – praise			
Base (similar to territory)			
Being needed			
Being of service			
Boredom			
Challenge			
Companionship			
Colleagues			
Contact with the public			
Contact with people with same skills			
Creativity			
Deadlines			
Disappointment			
Discipline			
Exercise			
Feedback			
Frustration			
Identity			
Income			

FACTORS IN JOB	FACTORS IN MY PRESENT JOB	I WANT TO KEEP (OR TO INCLUDE)	HOW CAN I FIND THEM IN FUTURE?
Independence			
Job satisfaction			
Knowledge			
Mental exertion			
Motivation			
Perks			
Physical exertion			
Physical strength			
Privacy			
Regular meals			
Role			
Routine			
Security			
Sense of belonging			
Sense of purpose			
Skills			
Social life			
Status			
Stress			
Structure of time			
Support			
Teamwork			
Territory			
Topics of conversation			
Travel (to work)			
Travel (in my work)			
Travel (world-wide)			
Vehicle			
Worry			
Younger people to work with			
Other			

Source: Changing Course, © Lifeskills Communications Ltd. First published as Branching Out. New edition published 1992 by Mercury Books, Gold Arrow Publications Ltd.

Exercise and meals may seem irrelevant to you. Remember the regular walk to the station or the number of corridors you walk down each day!

If you are considering self-employment, do recognise the importance of 'perks'. They may include typing and other office facilities; storage; tools; transport and other items you may take for granted.

What to do next: analyse your lists – remembering that there may be gaps in column 3 – How can I find them in future?

Make a note of those factors you want to eliminate from your future.

YOUR KNOWLEDGE AND EDUCATION

Think back to your time in education: school; college; training; later learning. What knowledge have you acquired? Think about the following questions and write down some notes on your recollections.

EXERCISE 2.3

What do you know?

When you were at school or in further training

1. What did you *enjoy*?

2. What did you *dislike*?

3. What were you *interested* in?

4. What were you *good* at?

5. What were you *less good* at?

6. Write about anything else that was *important* to you during your education and training?

Then you should:

- list the abilities, know-how, capabilities and aptitudes you acquired through education and learning; and

- make a record of details (date, institution etc.) of all your qualifications and training.

WHAT CAN YOU DO?

'I've always been in banking, I can't do anything else.'

'I'm just a housewife, I haven't any skills.'

'I left school at 15, I learned on the job.'

'I must stay in the advertising business, it's the only thing I can do.'

Do these remarks sound familiar to you? People of all ages, life stages and different occupations, and those presently working, unemployed or about to retire, all have muttered these or similar phrases as they face the prospect of changes in their lives. Like them, you share a common problem: you are thinking about only one kind of skill, namely: work content skills.

Work content skills are the specific, task-related skills which enable accountants to *calculate* balance sheets or typists to *manipulate* a typewriter. These are job content skills acquired through formal training, specialised knowledge and technical learning. Many work content skills require qualifications, leading to what we often call 'a skilled worker'.

But work content skills are only part of the story. If we dig a little deeper, we discover the vast reservoir of skills, experiences and abilities which can be transferred from one area of life to another. These transferable skills are often taken for granted, undervalued or ignored because we have never really needed to take note of them.

You have many transferable skills. You have been through 50+ years of living or, as it is known in professional circles, 'experiential learning'. You have talents, proficiencies, expertise and accomplishments: an assortment of natural knacks and skills which you may never have acknowledged before. These unsung and diploma-less abilities are vital in planning your future. And, understanding more about transferable skills will increase your self-marketing opportunities.

The skills exercise below looks at your transferable skills. It will assist you in identifying these strengths. It does not matter where you have acquired these skills: many will emerge from your employment and paid work, but others, just as valuable, are acquired through unpaid work (this includes domestic responsibilities, DIY, child care, caring for the infirm etc.), family, neighbourhood and community experiences and leisure time abilities.

Do not limit yourself by thinking only about those skills for which you have formal qualifications. This is your chance to do a little boasting. Come along, blow your own trumpet for a while and discover just how many special talents you have.

EXERCISE 2.4

What can you do?

Instructions: Consider each skill in turn. Fill in columns 1, 2 and 3 (not column 4 at this stage) according to the following scale:

1 = not at all
2 = a little
3 = average amount
4 = rather a lot
5 = very much

Add more skills to the end of the Skill Name column. If you need inspiration, check through the list of Action Verbs in Chapter 7.

When you have completed this part of the exercise, go over your list again and fill in column 4. Indicate where and how you can develop the skill. Use the following initials for paid work (PW), unpaid work (UW), education (E), training (T), leisure activities (LA), hobbies (H), community interests (CI).

	Column 1	*Column 2*	*Column 3*	*Column 4*
Skill Name	How much do you enjoy using this skill?	How competent are you at this skill?	How important is it for you to develop this skill?	Where and how can you develop this skill?
Analysing				
Assembling				
Brainstorming				
Budgeting				
Classifying				
Colour sense				
Composing – what?				
Computing				

Craft skills				
Creative thinking				
Creative writing				
Decision making				
Designing – what?				
Dexterity				
Diagnosing – what?				
Driving				
Foreign languages				
Green fingers				
Instructing				
Leading				
Listening				
Negotiating				
Observing				
Operating tools				
Persuading				
Precision work				
Problem solving				
Producing – what?				
Repairing				
Restoring				
Supervising				
Translating				
Welcoming				
Other skills				
Totals for each column:				

Then take the following steps.

1. Look at the **Totals** column: which has most ticks? What can you learn from this? Are you under or overvaluing your skills? Are there many skills in which you are proficient or few? Can you identify a group of skills where you have more or fewer skills?

2. Consider each column in turn and, using separate sheets, create four lists from each:

   List 1: all your highly proficient skills;

   List 2: all your adequate skills;

   List 3: skills you would like to develop;

   List 4: unimportant or irrelevant skills.

EXERCISE 2.5

What interests do you have?

Adults are usually excellent at identifying their interests. The list of interests here is adapted from 'Signposts', a card index system used in careers offices and libraries throughout the UK. If you would like to explore how your interests are linked to various careers, you will find 'Signposts' in your local careers office, either in card form or on a computerised system.

Read the categories below and answer the questions by listing your interests in order of priority, i.e. your most favoured interest at the top of the list. Note also how your interests may be linked to your skills in Exercise 2.3, which you filled in above.

	Yes	No
Arts/artistic Are you interested in drawing, painting, acting or other creative pursuits?		
Design Are you interested in drawings which can be used for making things?		

	Yes	No
Driving Are you interested in driving a vehicle?		
General service Are you interested in providing a general service directly to the public?		
Influencing/managing Are you interested in managing other people or influencing the way they think or act?		
Literary/verbal Are you interested in words, either writing or speaking?		
Mechanical/engineering Are you interested in making, using or repairing machinery or equipment?		
Natural Are you interested in looking after or using plants, animals or other natural resources?		
Numerical Are you interested in using numbers or working out mathematical problems?		
Outside Are you interested in being in the open air, either part or all of the time?		
Paperwork Are you interested in documents, files and letters?		
Practical Are you interested in using your hands or machinery to make, repair or otherwise treat things?		
Scientific/technical Are you interested in scientific and/or technical problems and their solutions?		
Social Service Are you interested in advising people and helping them with personal problems, including medical ones?		

PERSONAL QUALITIES

What are you like to work or be with – calm and unflappable or energetic and bursting with ideas? Are you an easygoing people person or a precise, task-oriented person? Are you practical and unemotional or imaginative and expressive? Are you conventional or independent, a rule-follower or a rebel?

In everyday life, we are always making informal predictions about other people, their characters and their temperaments. In choosing friends, colleagues, partners we make judgements about people, often based on our first impressions of that person. These are subjective evaluations, sometimes accurate but often mistaken.

Psychologists have a range of different methods with which to assess personality. These aim to be more objective and unbiased. Out of the many kinds of tests available to assess personality, the one most frequently used in career guidance is a personality inventory. It is not possible to reproduce any standardised questionnaires here as they are only available to qualified testers. If, however, you would like to try your hand at an enjoyable self-scoring questionnaire based on one of the world's leading indicators of personal style, the Myers-Briggs Type Indicator, have a look at the following books from Oxford Psychologists Press: *Please Understand Me* by David Keirsey and Marilyn Bates, *Type Talk* by Otto Kroeger and Janet M. Thusen and *Type Talk at Work* by Otto Kroeger and Janet M. Thusen (see Useful Addresses at the back of this book).

In the mean time use the following short quiz to help you describe your personal qualities now.

EXERCISE 2.6

What kind of person are you?

Follow these instructions:

- read each scale (pair of opposites) carefully;

- then, place one X (remember, only one X) on each line to represent the position that best describes you;

- try to avoid placing the X right in the middle of every dotted line – everyone has a few strong qualities;

Adaptable	.... /	Exact
Adventurous	.... /	Cautious
Argumentative	.... /	Harmonious
Compassionate	.... /	Firm
Conventional	.... /	Rebellious
Dynamic	.... /	Reflective
Emotional	.... /	Cool
Factual	.... /	Insightful
Follower	.... /	Leader
Gregarious	.... /	Reserved
Hi risk taker	.... /	Low risk taker
Honest	.... /	Forgetful
Independent	.... /	Conforming
Logical	.... /	Empathetic
Moody	.... /	Serene
Muddles along	.... /	Methodical
Open	.... /	Controlled
People person	.... /	Ideas person
Reliable	.... /	Changeable
Spontaneous	.... /	Orderly
Tough	.... /	Sensitive

Other qualities? Write them down here:

Now, using the scales as a guideline, write down a short **self-portrait** of yourself, using no more than 40 words.

USEFUL INFORMATION

This is not a definitive list, but represents just a few of the self-assessment books that are widely available. Many will be in your local public library.

- *Manage Your Own Career – a self-help guide for career planning*, by Ben Ball. Published by the British Psychological Society, St Andrews House, 48 Princess Road East, Leicester LE1 7DR.

- *What Colour is Your Parachute?* by Richard Bolles. This is an annual publication and is *the* American best-seller for job-seekers. Contains numerous exercises and skill inventories. Published by Ten Speed Press.

- *Build Your Own Rainbow. A Workbook for Career and Life Management*, by Barrie Hopson and Mike Scally, UK self-assessment for adults. Published by Mercury Books, Gold Arrow Publications Ltd.

- *Test Your Own Job Aptitude*, by J. Barrett and G. Williams, 2nd edn, published in 1990 by Kogan Page.

The Open University's Personal and Career Development Programme is a new study pack and course for adults incorporating a work-based project to develop transferable skills. It can be used by individuals, groups or as part of a corporate training programme and leads to a new OU Certificate award. For further information, contact The Enterprise in Higher Education Unit, The Open University, 10 Drumsheugh Gardens, Edinburgh EH3 7QL.

For women

- *Women Working it Out* and *It's Your Chance*, published by the Careers and Occupational Information Centre, Moorfoot, Sheffield S1 4PQ. Also available from local careers offices.

● *Springboard Women's Development Workbook*, by Liz Willis and Jenny Daisley. Published by Hawthorn Press.

CAREERS ADVICE

If you are still uncertain after completing these exercises, you may feel it would be helpful to discuss your career with an expert. There are two major types of career advice services – those who offer a psychological testing service and those who help with job hunting – but the distinction between the two may be hard to spot.

Psychological testing or vocational guidance agencies ask you to complete an in-depth personal information form, about your educational, occupational, family and present circumstances. You take a number of pencil and paper tests to measure your intelligence, aptitudes, personality and interests; some may be similar to the selection tests mentioned in Chapter 7. The tests may take up to half a day. Later, you will have a face-to-face interview with a consultant (usually an occupational psychologist), who will explain the results of the tests and discuss the options available to you.

Help with job hunting is more likely to be offered by career counsellors. They also offer testing, but the interview is usually longer and broadly based; it may even cover several sessions. Help may also include CV preparation, interview rehearsal, information resources (education, training, professional journals) and job search techniques. There is only a small difference between some career counsellors and outplacement specialists: both may suggest they have access to the 'hidden' employment market and hint at finding you a job. Take care with these promises: no one can guarantee you a job and it does not necessarily follow that higher fees produce more successful work.

There are pros and cons to all these services, which are usually fee-paying and mainly London based. Vocational guidance will not find you a job and may include tests which are really super-fluous to your needs at this life stage. After all, do you really need to know your IQ now or discover a hidden aptitude for mechanics? Career counselling guarantees nothing and could be very time consuming. On the 'plus' side, tests may prevent you from making a disastrous mistake or confirm your own judgement about a career change. It is often very helpful to have someone objective with whom to discuss your future. All career advice, with a few exceptions, has a mixed reputation. You may well ask yourself: how can I avoid wasting my money?

American job-hunting expert writer, Richard Bolles, suggests 'the three things you absolutely want from anyone you're paying good money to is . . . a firm grasp of the whole job-hunting process, at its most creative and effective level; the ability to communicate information lucidly and clearly, [and] rapport with you.' Here are some further guidelines.

- Ask for a free, introductory, no-obligation talk before signing up.

- Find out exactly what the career counsellor will do. Explain what you want and listen to their answers.

- Discover if the agency has a specialist orientation. Some services work mainly with middle managers, redundant executives or youngsters. (There's nothing wrong with any of these, but I think you should know before signing up.) If you are not in these groups, you may not feel comfortable.

- Find out who will be counselling you and their qualifications; how much one-to-one time you will have; the exact fees; if there is a comprehensive written and/or taped report; and if follow-up sessions are available.

- Will you take a battery of tests? If so, what will the tests measure? Are they appropriate for your situation? Is skills analysis provided – from all areas of life, paid and non-paid work? (This is very important for anyone re-entering the workplace after a career gap, especially those with domestic and family responsibilities, or late starters.)

- Is the tester qualified? The British Psychological Society maintains a members' Register of Competence in Occupational Testing (RCOT). Tel.: 0533 549568.

- Take care with advisers who are vague or communicate poorly; talk about past clients (professional ethics require complete confidentiality); imply that over 50s should be put out to grass or a degree is the answer to everything (it isn't).

- Avoid having your CV prepared by the agency. Instead, look for guidance in how to prepare and adapt it yourself.

- Do not sign up for telephone career advice or postal help. Unless you require a specific piece of information (name and address of an institution, for example), it is insufficient.

- Go for the counsellor who expects you both to work together and inspires confidence; makes you feel positive and hopeful, yet realistic. Look favourably towards someone who will guide and support you to help yourself.

Free career advice may be available from your local careers office (look in your local phone book or *Thomson* directory). In general, careers offices focus mainly on school leavers, but several are available to adults. Avoid busy times (Easter, June, July and August) and telephone first for an appointment. Even if individual help is unavailable, the careers office's information resources (leaflets, publications, computer-based information) with its Careers and Occupational Information Centre (COIC) should be open to you. Details about free educational guidance services for adults (EGSAs) can be found at local public libraries, Citizens' Advice Bureaux and in reference books such as *Second Chances*. An *Adult Guidance Directory* is available from the Institute of Careers Guidance. See Useful Addresses.

Fee-paying career services advertise in *Yellow Pages*, books, newspapers and magazines. Qualified professionals include members of the British Psychological Society or the Institute of Careers Guidance. Private guidance costs vary and it is impossible to give fixed guidelines here, apart from suggesting you compare several brochures and fee scales. If you live far from sources of help, or are homebound, ask for an outreach worker: there are not many around, but you may strike lucky!

Will a career agency help you? Of course, everyone is different, but I do know how my own life was given a jolt by career guidance. When my elder daughter was unsure about her A level choices, but reluctant to have professional vocational help, I persuaded her towards it. 'I'll go along if you will,' I said. The result? She came away less than happy (well, have you ever heard of a teenager taking notice of commonsense!) but I was thoroughly astounded. 'You have an "uneducated" brain', wrote the consultant psychologist. 'I must emphasise that you undoubtedly have the necessary aptitudes to cope with further and higher studies . . .'

Career guidance changed my life, but even if it does not work so well for you, the very minimum you can expect is a clearer knowledge of your strengths and resources. If, in addition, you gain a professional, unbiased estimation of your occupational and personal development and a better understanding of your choices for the future, then, I believe, it is a worthwhile investment.

3

Wage/Salary Work

THIS CHAPTER CONTAINS DETAILS of wage or salary work, paying special attention to those jobs which value experience and maturity. This is not a complete list – many fields appreciate the older worker's skills and knowledge – but the following represents a selection of opportunities where age is either an advantage or is irrelevant. You may wish to consider other occupations, depending on your personal situation, past training and future demands.

It is also useful to know where not to look for work. Generally speaking, older workers should avoid jobs with a large physical component – for example, it is extremely unlikely that you will become a professional ballet dancer in your 50s! Neither is it a good idea to start very extensive training or a long apprenticeship as employers will not be able to gain sufficient benefit from your services after qualification. This is not the time to take up brain surgery!

Close alternative careers may exist. If you cannot become a dental surgeon, you could train to become a dental technician or dental surgery assistant. It is also worth noting that, in some jobs, long service as an assistant may count towards qualifying as a professional, i.e. legal executives, after the required amount of experience and taking some exams, may become solicitors.

Even if there is an upper age limit for the job you want, do not give up hope. Age limits may be unofficially more flexible, so make enquiries. Read everything you can get your hands on. See if you can arrange work 'shadowing' sessions, that is spending time alongside an experienced employee, observing the job.

61

Occasionally it may lead to a job offer. Look at access courses and training for mature entrants (see Chapter 6) or find out if you could attend a course without taking examinations. If, after all that, you feel you have the talents and temperament, and there is a demand for employees – try your luck . . . you have nothing whatsoever to lose.

Below you will find information on the types of work you could consider. Details are listed under six headings (which are omitted if not relevant to the section).

1. **Is this for you?**   A brief overview of the work.

2. **Particularly suitable for**   Details of previous jobs or experience here where relevant.

3. **Training**   Here you will find information about where to find updating or training courses, ideally of one year's duration only.

4. **Market possibilities**   Financial rewards are indicated by low/medium/high. Suggested job vacancies are included.

5. **Rewards and restraints**   These are some pros and cons of the work – what you may like about the job, what may be drawbacks.

6. **Useful information**   Contact details and/or relevant publications. Remember to enclose a stamped addressed envelope to the organisations listed in this section.

EXECUTIVES/SENIOR MANAGERS

Independent management

Essentially, temporary or interim managers are self-employed, but the work is included here for those who intend making a serious commitment to long-term independent practice by setting up their own company. Their own company, therefore, will pay them a salary.

(I am indebted to Nigel Corby, General Manager, CBI/P-E International, Egham, Surrey for his generous contribution to this section.)

1. **Is this for you?**   Temporary, or interim, managers cover gaps in organisations to deal with specific project requirements. These are experienced, carefully focused individuals, strongly motivated to succeed and able to concentrate fully on the requirements of the task. They do not waste time settling in – instead, they grasp problems or market challenges swiftly, sensibly and cost-effectively with no arguments when the job is done.

2. **Particularly suitable for**   Making the choice for independence requires a bold decision. You must be efficient, thorough and effective, not only in your dealings with individual clients, but also in the eyes of companies who may wish to engage your services and the agencies who may provide you with business.

   You are best suited to this work style if you are 'sensibly over-qualified': that is, with proven relevant skills and high quality experience. You should be able to demonstrate about ten years' experience at the top of your particular tree in companies with a minimum of £5 million turnover. You will also be required by the better agencies to show a commitment to independent practice by setting up a limited company and illustrate a professional approach to developing your business.

   It is essential to make a whole-hearted commitment to self-employment. Set yourself up either as a sole trader or as a limited company (see Chapter 5) and create a positive marketing image for your services, taking specialist advice where necessary.

4. **Market possibilities**   Interim managers are particularly effective in the management of change, during an acquisition or shut down, relocation, merger or flotation. Several agencies have sprung up to give corporate clients access to the pool of temporary managers. Those agencies allied to the

Association of Temporary and Interim Executive Services operate a strict code of conduct ensuring the highest quality standards. To register with an agency, you must meet their requirements of seniority, independence and skills; you should contact them initially and expect to be carefully interviewed before any introduction to a client company. Average assignments last for three to six months and require flexible fee arrangements with no 'hidden' extras. Integrity and confidentiality are of paramount importance.

It is less than sensible to rely on agencies entirely. Although you will probably be on the books of several, you should also take every opportunity to find your own clients – this will enhance your reputation both with organisations and agencies. Register with several key agencies rather than one, but shun anyone who asks for a fee to enter their network. For example, CBI/P-E International do not charge interim managers for entry on to their data base; equally, they give no guarantees for future work.

Market your company – not yourself – suggests Corby, and emphasise the quality of the service you can offer: flexibility, concentrated effort, high motivation, fast start, cost-effectiveness and ability to see a job through to completion.

Finally, here is another tip: do not use a personal CV to market your services. Corby describes those lengthy technical specifications full of in-jargon as 'yawnmakers'. Much better, he suggests, is a brochure clearly focused on your company's skills. Aim to increase your company's business, not yourself; that's the way to make sure you are busy.

5. **Rewards and restraints** There are some management executives who consider those outside the full-time employment system as strange, unfortunate and without much to offer. These are serious misconceptions because, during the last decade or two, there are very few managers who have not had to change track due to economic or industrial change. Of course, any workforce will have its share of less than competent employees. Those who have chosen to work as independent managers are vital, dynamic and resourceful

professionals, not merely misfits just trying to find something to do.

If you are considering setting up as an independent temporary executive, Nigel Corby offers this advice: first, be aware this is a courageous career choice. 'Temporary' or 'interim' does not mean filling in time between one full-time job and another. If you have taken early retirement or been made redundant after years in a senior management position, ask yourself if you really want to return to what Corby aptly describes as the 'corporate overcoat'. Many firms are working with minimal teams these days, in an effort to reduce overheads. Those presently in organisational employment face uncertainty, stress and strain, while several are overstretched to the point of inefficiency. And the chances of improvement in the future are not promising. Ask yourself: is this the climate in which you wish to spend the next 15 or more years of your working life? If you answer 'No', then consider interim management.

6. Useful information
CBI/P-E International, Park House, Wick Road, Egham, Surrey TW20 0HW.

Association of Temporary and Interim Executive Services, 36/38 Mortimer Street, London W1N 7RB.

Also, see Chapter 4: British Executive Service Overseas; Public Appointments Unit; Non-executive directorships.

HOUSING/PROPERTY

Housing management

1. Is this for you? Housing managers provide and manage rented accommodation, interviewing and selecting tenants, dealing with rent arrears, arranging repairs and consulting with tenants' groups. They also have dealings with social workers. With recent changes, housing managers may also be involved with rent rebate schemes, housing research, formulating policy and running aid centres. Property managers often act as caretakers for absentee owners or for holiday accommodation. The work is broad based – in some cases, you just keep an eye on the place and pay the bills; in others, you may be required to take on housekeeping services or at least supervise domestic staff.

2. **Particularly suitable for**   You need to be able to deal with people. Housing managers may have to deal with problem or unruly tenants, so firmness combined with tolerance is essential. Private property managers may need foreign languages.

3. **Training**   Social work, accountancy, general management, social administration are all background possibilities, but professional diplomas may be less important than life experience. Relevant work is useful.

4. **Market possibilities**   Housing managers usually work for local authorities, but there is an increase in the numbers of housing associations. Try building societies, property companies and charitable trusts. Property managers should make themselves known to estate agents and international companies. Pay: medium.

5. **Rewards and restraints**   If you can be diplomatic early in the morning or late at night, this may be for you! These jobs require charm at anti-social hours. Returners and the 'temporarily retired' are welcome to take housing management refresher courses and workshops. Work is mainly office based, although private property managers may find themselves running around after casual and maintenance staff.

6. **Useful information**
The Institute of Housing, Octavia House,
Westwood Business Park, Westwood Way, Coventry CV4 8JP.

Tenant liaison work

1. **Is this for you?** A recently created occupation, tenant liaison officers supplement the work of housing managers. Work involves overseeing a patch of properties and interviewing potential tenants, allocating available housing, rent collection and arrears chasing, tenant welfare and support.

2. **Particularly suitable for** those with practical experience of the work. Voluntary work acceptable.

3. **Training** Unnecessary, but qualifications such as BTEC Housing Studies useful.

4. **Market possibilities** Employers range from local authorities, high street estate agents, building societies, property companies, housing associations and organisations such as Shelter.

6. **Useful information**
Housing Careers Service, 2 Valentine Place, London SE1 8QH.

FINANCIAL SERVICES

If you possess accountancy or similar financial skills, you are fortunate. Your services are in demand in a number of new appointments; for example, the recently created hospital trusts require financial managers; bursars are needed for newly independent schools, further education colleges and housing associations. The accountancy body specialising in public sector work, the Chartered Institute of Public Finance and Accounting, has a training scheme for accountants, emphasising practical finance relevant to specific fields of employment – for example, working in a hospital. This scheme will be open to others, including school leavers and the unemployed. Contact: CIPFA, 3 Robert Street, London WC2N 6BH.

Insurance and investment

1. **Is this for you?** Insurance companies welcome mature applicants, particularly for sales representative work. Insurance sales staff work outside the office; they bring in new business and, as home service agents, deal directly by visiting people in their homes, collecting premiums and explaining policies. Loss adjusters often transfer from other fields to handling claims between clients and insurers. Investment advisers, as agents for companies, help clients plan their finances using their employers' products.

2. **Particularly suitable for** Sales/marketing experience not necessary but useful; understanding of money and maths; thorough and methodical. Selling insurance is a people job, so communication skills needed.

3. **Training** Sales representatives usually train on the job; loss adjusters also train in-house, plus part-time study available from the Chartered Institute of Loss Adjusters.

4. **Market possibilities** Good opportunities especially for those who dress smartly and conservatively. Look at local insurance brokers, major companies and specialist loss adjusting firms. Think about a selected market – grandchildren, inheritance, disability, health. Take care over pay – commission only is commonplace.

5. **Rewards and restraints** Flexible patterns of work are possible with part-time jobs and working from home being popular options. You cannot set yourself up as an independent financial adviser or take employment with a firm unless you are authorised by FIMBRA (Financial Intermediaries, Managers and Brokers Regulatory Association) or a similar regulatory body, such as the Institute of Chartered Accountants. FIMBRA is the principal insurance services industry 'watchdog'.

6. **Useful information**
The Chartered Insurance Institute, 20 Aldermanbury, London EC2V 7HY.

The Chartered Institute of Loss Adjusters, 376 Strand, London WC2R 0LR.

FIMBRA, Hartsmere House, Hartsmere Road, London E14 4AB.

Tax preparation

In the USA, many older workers go into tax preparation, that is, charging people to prepare their personal tax return. Most Americans seem to hate the task and are willing to pay someone else to do it for them. Self-assessed tax returns will be introduced in the UK from 1996/7, and so there is every possibility this second career will take hold here. Look for details in the 1994 Finance Act. If you are good with numbers and people, keep up with tax regulations and allowances, and can inspire enough confidence in others for them to reveal their financial affairs to you – get ready to start as soon as legislation is passed. Be prepared!

Legal cashiers

1. **Is this for you?** Being a financial expert within the legal profession provides lawyers with the back-up which solicitors need to run their business. Legal cashiers are responsible for keeping various accounts, investing moneys from trusts or deposits on properties, administering the practice's books. In a big firm, this can amount to many thousands of pounds and thus become complex. There are strict rules laid down by the Law Society about how solicitors' accounts should be organised.

2. **Particularly suitable for** Those with financial and/or secretarial experience. Bookkeeping, budgeting and business planning experience useful.

3. **Training** No full-time courses; various correspondence courses – details from addresses below.

4. **Market possibilities** Law firms, legal centres. Some freelance work possible. Pay: medium.

5. **Rewards and restraints** Chasing after busy solicitors to obtain their detailed time sheets in order to assess fees etc. may need tact and diplomacy! The range of work depends on the size of the firm: in a large practice, you may be able to specialise in one aspect of the work, say probate, but in a smaller practice, you may have to manage everything. Computer familiarity is increasingly required.

6. **Useful information**
The Institute of Legal Executives, Kempston Manor, Kempston, Bedford MK42 7AB.

The Institute of Legal Cashiers and Administrators, 136 Well Hall Road, Eltham, London SE9 6SN.

The Institute of Legal Accounts Managers, Stone House, 275–7 Greenwich High Road, London SE10 8NB.

Fund-raising

Many organisations employ fund-raising personnel at executive, organiser and field level. You could be responsible for every aspect of an appeal – a school, for example, may engage an appeals director who will plan, administer and carry out everything from a gala event to face-to-face visits. Generally, this will be fee-based work. Salaried jobs include corporate appeals executives, promotion organisers, regional and area field staff and supervisors. Integrity is absolutely essential, as is some previous track record of success. Market possibilities include churches, hospitals, schools, non-profit organisations.

Other possibilities

Company secretary (if you have professional qualifications in law or accountancy); building societies; postal work (in head post offices or main branch offices), mailroom management in companies; sub-postmaster.

COURT STAFF

Judges' clerks

1. **Is this for you?**   Judges' clerks are personal assistants for individual judges. They work alongside their judge, travelling with them on circuit and providing them with personal, organisational and secretarial support.

2. **Particularly suitable for**   Some experience as a personal assistant in commerce useful; word processing skills now essential.

3. **Training**   On the job.

4. **Market possibilities**   Vacancies are advertised nationally; usually one intake per year. Application forms can be obtained from the address below. Upper age limits do not exist for this work. In order to offer a reasonable period of service, you should apply at least a couple of years – preferably more – before you reach statutory retirement age. Pay: medium.

5. **Rewards and restraints**   If you enjoy smoothing the path for someone, this is for you. You will type reports and correspondence, carry books and papers to and from the court, maintain the Judge's robes in good condition – and assist with robing. Away from home, you will co-operate with local authorities, the police and others – all in all, this is a status occupation as long as you are content always to be the bridesmaid!

6. **Useful information**
   The Lord Chancellor's Department, Central Recruiting Unit, Rochester House, 33 Greycoat Street, London SW1P 2QS.

Court ushers

Court ushers are also appointed by The Lord Chancellor's Department, Central Recruiting Unit, for London, or by the

Local Court Administrative Office out of London (consult your local Town Hall for details). Duties include ushering witnesses in and out of the court and dealing with paperwork. No prior qualifications are necessary and age limits are the same as for judges' clerks (60/63). Training is on the job. This is a flexible job as the work can be part-time or full-time. As with most jobs involving other people, you need to be bright and sociable, with an interest in the court. Indeed, a recent juror, having finished a term of jury service, applied successfully to become a court usher. Vacancies are sometimes advertised in the local press, if it is a small court, or at Job Centres.

Justices' clerks and Justices' clerks' assistants

1. **Is this for you?** If you have either solicitors' or barristers' qualifications, but do not wish to practise law, you may like to consider advising and assisting lay magistrates (JPs) as a justices' clerk. The work is advisory: the clerk may sit in the court and hear cases, then guide the bench on the law.

   Without any qualifications (although GCSEs are preferred), you can become a justices' clerks' assistant by preparing summonses and warrants, issuing licences, dealing with fines and procedural matters.

2. **Particularly suitable for** Anyone who is discreet, honest and trustworthy. Law qualifications are essential for clerks.

3. **Training** Training given by the Home Office.

4. **Market possibilities** As for judges' clerks.

5. **Rewards and restraints** There is close contact with the public, many of whom may be under considerable stress. At times, clerks' offices are frantically busy.

Other possibilities

The Crown Prosecution Service (CPS) employs an extensive back-up team to assist lawyers and carry out the many administrative tasks for the court. Similar to civil service appointments, staff are graded and, after experience, may go on to specialise. Law clerks, clerical officers, legal assistants and similar posts are people-oriented jobs with variety, interest and challenge. All CPS employees retire at 60 years of age and there is a top entry age for legal trainees of 55 years. If you are in your early 50s, this area is well worth considering. Enquiries to: The Crown Prosecution Service, 50 Ludgate Hill, London EC4M 7EX.

LEGAL

Legal executive (not Scotland)

1. **Is this for you?**   The demand for para-legals should increase as the Lord Chancellor's reform of the legal system gets under way. One major change is to encourage the use of professionally qualified legal executives. Legal executives work under solicitors preparing documents, researching details and interviewing. They often possess a specialist knowledge of conveyancing, probate, litigation or commercial law. Sometimes they deal with accounts and train junior staff.

2. **Particularly suitable for**   Patient, persevering people, able to cope with detail and able to concentrate for long periods. Legal secretaries often take Institute of Legal Executive (ILEX) examinations as a career advancement.

3. **Training**   Part-time training alongside everyday work. After qualification and experience, legal executives may become solicitors (part-time courses are presently under discussion with the Law Society).

4. **Market possibilities**   Most para-legals work for solicitors; fewer are employed by the Civil Service, local government, commerce and industry. Also try benefit shops, legal advice and community centres. Advantageous to have an area of

expertise: social security, housing and European law are examples. Pay: medium–high.

5. **Rewards and restraints** Dealing with clients who may be upset and anxious demands tact and calm. Previous relevant experience makes job finding smoother, but is not a requirement for training.

6. **Useful information**
The Institute of Legal Executives, Kempston Manor, Kempston, Bedford MK42 7AB.

Other possibilities

Dealing with the transfer of property used to be the bread and butter of solicitors' practices. Now, licensed conveyancers are permitted to do this work (but not in Scotland) and are recognised independent professionals. They work on their own, in local government or solicitors' offices. Information from The Secretary, Council for Licensed Conveyancers, Golden Cross House, Duncannon Street, London WC2N 4JF.

CLERICAL/ADMINISTRATION

Secretarial

1. **Is this for you?** For many years, secretarial work has been the mainstay of the, especially female, workforce. Girls were advised to learn shorthand and typing in order to fill the gap between school and marriage, and as a skill which would 'always come in useful'. As office equipment changed, many secretarial jobs began to disappear. Today, the traditional typist with only basic skills has more or less vanished. This is due not only to computerisation, but also to greater use of temporary, part-time and freelance staff, and the changes in office structure: while firms are reducing the numbers of

support and administrative staff, they also expect employees to be more flexible in their work. The top secretary of the 1990s may play a number of higher level roles: communications co-ordinator, projects manager, conference organiser, business supervisor. And all this in addition to excellent English and numeracy, fast and accurate keyboard/word processing skills, shorthand, good telephone manner and possibly a foreign language or two.

2. **Particularly suitable for** These days, secretarial work is available for men as well as women who are well spoken, adaptable, tactful and discreet. The best jobs go to those skilled in using modern equipment, who demonstrate enthusiasm and unflappability. Past experience in medical, legal, agricultural and financial fields is useful.

3. **Training** If you are returning to secretarial work after a career gap, take an updating course. Newcomers aiming for senior jobs should look for secretarial courses which include business administration (banking, marketing, sales), as well as technical skills. Brush up any foreign languages.

4. **Market possibilities** There is ongoing demand for expert secretaries in all fields. Some advertisements (and employment agencies) appear uninterested in mature applicants, but, take heart – a careful scrutiny of vacancies indicates that more and more firms are recognising the advantages of the older person. If the 'preferred' age states 40 or 45 years, go for it!

5. **Rewards and restraints** In the past, it was hard to move up the organisational hierarchy from secretarial level. Now, career development is much more likely, although competition is intense. Companies welcome new, unemployed graduates who perceive secretarial work as a stepping stone into permanent, managerial posts. A specialism increases an older worker's chance of success.

6. **Useful information**
Institute of Qualified Private Secretaries, 126 Farnham Road, Slough, Berks SL1 4HA.

JOBS FOR THE OVER 50S

Medical secretaries

Medical secretaries are always in demand, as personal assistants to consultants, in hospitals, laboratories, private clinics, general practice, public health, drug companies and as practice administrators. Specialist courses are available from the Association of Medical Secretaries, Practice Administrators and Receptionists, Tavistock House North, Tavistock Square, London WC1H 9LN.

Red tape

If you have been a local authority employee or a civil servant and find yourself looking for work, consider switching your experience to the private sector. One 50-ish ex-governmental development official took early retirement, had a short holiday and immediately set about turning his experience into a valuable asset as director of a professional association. He could have also looked at trade unions, regulatory boards, and national or pressure groups. How could you turn your career around? If you have been a benefits officer, could you shift into personnel work or retirement planning? Consider a related field: financial advice; insurance sales. Also, look at opportunities in advising private business on how to handle red tape – and doing it for them. If you were in town planning, think how valuable you could be to a development company!

RETAILING

Book selling

1. **Is this for you?** It always delights me to go to our local book shop where the owner is knowledgeable and helpful. Often, I find the very book I have looked for desperately everywhere else or, when I'm really not sure what it is I require, having the time and personal attention of an interested proprietor.

Bookselling is retail trading, subject to all the ups and downs of commerce and the fierce competition of chain stores.

2. **Particularly suitable for** Anyone with commercial sense plus a good memory, people, bookkeeping and teamwork skills, patience with diffident/difficult customers.

3. **Training** Mainly on the job, but certificate courses are available and some are distance learning.

4. **Market possibilities** Working for an established book shop is a sensible first step before setting up your own. Any retail operation requires a solid financial footing, since book suppliers want a good credit rating for accounts. Choose your area very carefully; those in the know recommend a middle-class site.

5. **Rewards and restraints** A love of books is essential but you need more: highly skilled buying, good customer skills, accurate record keeping and stock control. Specialised knowledge is needed for children's bookshops, with good contacts at schools, parents' associations etc.

   Seasonal work is available in book shops, prior to Christmas. Lifting piles of books around the shop is not for those with bad backs, however!

6. **Useful information**
The Booksellers' Association of Great Britain and Ireland, 272 Vauxhall Bridge Road, London SW1V 1BA.

Antiques

1. **Is this for you?** Antique dealers tend to specialise either in large pieces of furniture or smaller 'collectibles' and jewellery. Both tend to be occupations which people drift into following an interest or hobby. Sometimes they start with interesting pieces of their own, perhaps collected over many years; at other times they have developed a 'knack' for bargain spotting which leads them into trading. You can deal from home, a shop, a covered market stall, a kiosk, even a car boot. At the top end of the antiques trade, there are the

big London shops and auction houses which are good places to learn about prices and sales techniques. You will spend a lot of time talking to people: other dealers, browsing customers, museum and gallery staff, trade fair exhibitors.

2. **Particularly suitable for**   Practically anyone with enough know-how; haggling experience very useful.

3. **Training**   There are no formal training courses for dealing in antiques, but you need a good knowledge of art and history. Fine art courses are available; workshops, lectures and evening classes also.

4. **Market possibilities**   Stock comes from house clearances, auction houses, other dealers, private vendors. Specialise in a particular period or type of collection.

5. **Rewards and restraints**   Market stalls are for the fit and healthy, especially in winter or when pitched near the door. Eyes in the back of your head are an advantage, too, if you carry many small items on display. Cash flow needs attention as you may have to carry stock for some time before making a sale. Trade gazettes and collectors' guides are useful, but experienced dealers say you should not depend on them. Join a trade association when experienced. Not for those with two left feet!

6. **Useful information**
London & Provincial Antique Dealers' Association,
535 King's Road, London SW10 0SZ.

Estate agent

1. **Is this for you?**   Estate agents in the USA – or realtors, as they are called there – are mainly mature adults, often mid-stage women. At present in the UK, there is a youthful approach to finding buyers for properties, but as our population ages, so may estate agents. Of course, like many other businesses, the property market is subject to market conditions, but there are always – even in the worst of times –

people who must move home and thus require estate agency services.

2. **Particularly suitable for** Those with sales experience and flair; past business experience useful.

3. **Training** Not essential unless you want to do professional surveys or give financial advice.

4. **Market possibilities** Openings for people offering specialised services: for example, wealthy or highly mobile/ international clients requiring agents able to see the entire process through from start to finish. Contact embassies, national corporations, relocation consultants. Fee-based pay, commission usual.

5. **Rewards and restraints** If you get on well with people from all age groups, are diplomatic, persuasive and convincing, estate agency work is fulfilling. Good negotiating and liaison skills are required for dealing with vendors as well as buyers. Try developing a specialist service, such as restoring older properties (you will need to know about historic houses, damp proofing, modernisation etc.) or interior decorating and furnishing.

6. **Useful information**
National Association of Estate Agents, 21 Jury Street, Warwick CV34 4EH.

HEALTH AND SAFETY

Inspectors

1. **Is this for you?** This work is concerned with the health, safety and welfare of people at work and the public who may be affected by work activities. Health and safety inspectors are often called in to deal with disasters, but their main tasks are to visit any workplace from factories to hospitals,

construction sites to offices and shops, ensuring machinery, equipment and conditions meet legal requirements.

2. **Particularly suitable for** Professional graduates such as engineers, with industrial experience, and a clean driving licence. Maths useful. Academic qualifications are not always necessary.

3. **Training** Some training is on the job, depending on previous track record. Post-graduate programmes are available, as is some distance learning.

4. **Market possibilities** An expanding field with good opportunities for full-time, part-time, job-sharing.

5. **Rewards and restraints** Health and safety inspectors travel away from their offices several days weekly. They need to be able to get on well with all sorts of people, who may, sometimes, be in distress or disgruntled. Specialist inspectors deal with railways, mines, nuclear plants. Agricultural inspectors work with agriculture, horticulture and forestry.

6. **Useful information**
Health and Safety Executive, St Hugh's House,
Stanley Precinct, Bootle, Merseyside L20 3QY.

MEDICAL

Dispensing optician

1. **Is this for you?** Dispensing opticians only dispense prescriptions for spectacles, contact lenses and other appliances, but do not test eye sight or examine eyes. They discuss frames and lenses with patients, and also deal in a variety of optical apparatus – sunglasses, for example.

2. **Particularly suitable for** Those with manual dexterity, a liking for precision work, sales experience and people skills. Science graduates may gain some exemptions.

3. **Training** Full-time, day release and correspondence courses available. Upper age limit is only related to a person's ability to study.

4. **Market possibilities** As most adults require spectacles for reading from their 40s onwards, this work is expected to grow as the population ages. The numbers of high street stores have increased dramatically in recent years. Pay: medium.

5. **Rewards and restraints** There is a lot of customer contact, fixed salary and hours, and all the advantages of indoor work. Possible job-sharing and career development into shop management.

6. **Useful information**
The Association of British Dispensing Opticians,
6 Hurlingham Business Park, Sullivan Road,
London SW6 3DU.

Alternative medicine

Recent years have seen an increase of interest in alternatives to conventional medicine and, as a result, there has been growth in the practitioners of chiropractice, acupuncture, homoeopathy and other branches of complementary techniques. It is not possible here to describe each one in detail. Instead, this section offers some general guidelines for those considering training and practising these occupations.

1. **Is this for you?** Acupuncturists treat illness by inserting special needles into various specified locations in a person's body. Chiropractors specialise in treating spinal pain with manipulation, while osteopaths treat all mechanical parts of the body to restore normal function. Hypnotherapy is often taken up by older people with life experience; they use hypnosis as a method to treat conditions controlled by the unconscious. Homoeopathy, perhaps the best-respected of the alternative approaches, heals illness by taking a holistic view of disease, treating the whole patient with minute doses of drugs on the principle that like cures like.

2. **Particularly suitable for**   People with an interest and background in science and medicine; compassion, dedication and self-confidence are core personal qualities.

3. **Training**   Courses vary in length and quality. Take care to register only with training establishments which meet the requirements of the Institute of Complementary Medicine's Register.

4. **Market possibilities**   Demand continues to increase. Recommendation by other professionals is best. Hourly fees, medium income.

5. **Rewards and restraints**   At present, there are no statutory regulations for complementary practitioners, so you could face difficulties from local orthodox medics. Most practitioners are in private practice, working from home and/or from consulting rooms at a centre alongside others. Some equipment may be required, although hypnotherapists require only a comfortable chair or couch. A few (chiropractors, acupuncturists) work alongside GPs in medical practices. Chiropractors are officially recognised in many other countries, but NHS recognition in the UK is awaited.

6. **Useful information**
Institute for Complementary Medicine,
PO Box 194, London SE16 1QZ.

Dietician/dietary therapist

1. **Is this for you?**   Dieticians work with doctors to plan menus for hospital patients and others who need special diets. They also work with various groups within the community, explaining the importance of diet and nutrition, and how diets can be managed at home. Some are involved in research and teaching, manufacturing new products, carrying out surveys, working in the media or as consultants. More recently, dieticians have broadened their jobs to include health education and preventive work. Dietary therapists also prescribe diets, to treat and prevent illness, but, as a

newer occupation, the work is closer to complementary or alternative medicine. In particular, dietary therapists treat cases where conventional medicine has been ineffective.

2. **Particularly suitable for** Practical people, ideally with a nursing or biology background, with an interest in science; good and persuasive communicators, able to give presentations, lectures etc.

3. **Training** Mature students are accepted on all courses. Post-graduate diplomas are available for those with relevant background. Diploma courses are available for dietary therapists.

4. **Market possibilities** There is no age-bar in these jobs. Look for openings in hospitals, medical and community centres, alternative health practices, natural health groups. Freelance work available; also part-time and job sharing. Income range is low/medium.

5. **Reward and restraints** As interest in what we eat has increased during recent times, dietary advice has changed from a narrow, specialised occupation to a broader, more visible occupation. Dieticians can choose from a variety of jobs: such as managing catering services in organisations, keeping social workers and medical personnel up to date or advising the elderly.

6. **Useful information**
British Dietetic Association, 7th Floor, Elizabeth House, Queensway, Birmingham B1 1LS.

Dietary Therapy Association, 210 Tufnell Park Road, London N7 0PZ.

Sex therapist

1. **Is this for you?** Sex therapists help people overcome ignorance and sexual tensions caused by physical, mental or emotional problems. It is very likely to be a second or later career, a specialist area of counselling (see below) described

as one which is 'talky-talky, *not* feely-feely'! Clients may come for help alone or as a couple. They may be experiencing specific difficulties following surgery (mastectomy, for example), illness or require more general help with their relationship. It is important for sex therapists to inspire confidence in their clients as well as those who may refer clients to them. Qualifications and training, although not strictly essential, are highly recommended.

2. **Particularly suitable for**   About 20 per cent of sex therapists have a medical background – obstetricians, gynaecologists, general practitioners – while a further 20 per cent come from nursing. Others come from various other settings including religious workers, social work, psychology and counselling.

3. **Training**   Part-time certificate and diploma courses from British Association for Sexual and Marital Therapy, and Relate.

4. **Market possibilities**   Doctors, marriage guidance centres, hospitals, family planning units, HIV and AIDS clinics. Income: medium–low.

5. **Rewards and restraints**   Medical personnel are sometimes surprised by the training, which is less physiological than they expected. The work requires self-awareness and insight, and is best for those with broad-minded views on race, religion, creed and sexual practice. Can be a home-based occupation, an income supplement or a mix of salary and freelance.

6. **Useful information**
British Association for Sexual and Marital Therapy,
PO Box 62, Sheffield S10 3TS.

Relate (National Marriage Council), Little Church Street, Rugby, Warwickshire CV21 3AP.

Psychotherapy and counselling

1. **Is this for you?** Psychotherapists and counsellors are always mature adults with work or life experience. There is on-going

confusion about these occupations, as both have several meanings. To simplify matters, psychotherapists usually treat individuals with psychological or emotional problems, whereas counsellors' work, in general, involves helping 'normal' people discuss their personal problems. There are various 'schools' of psychotherapy, and forms of treatment (usually in medical settings) vary greatly. Counselling is often part of another job, such as social work, probation service, personnel. Generally speaking, counsellors are not as highly qualified as fully trained psychotherapists.

2. **Particularly suitable for** *Psychotherapy:* those with medical or psychology qualifications; previous personal analysis sometimes necessary. *Counselling:* teachers, social workers, personnel, welfare. Past experience less important than open-mindedness, warmth and patience.

3. **Training** At present, anyone – without any qualifications whatsoever – can set themselves up as a psychotherapist or counsellor. But you are strongly advised against this. Even if you think you are well suited because you enjoyed a workshop or two, or you have solved your own or other people's problems for many years – do not be tempted. Professional accreditation for psychotherapists and counsellors is essential to protect both clients and practitioners. The addresses below offer details of recognised training. Some counselling training is available through voluntary bodies, such as the Samaritans.

4. **Market possibilities** Psychotherapists are usually employed by hospitals, voluntary agencies or are in private practice. Counsellors work with schools, colleges, voluntary groups, NHS practices and advice agencies. Specialist areas are common, such as ethnic minorities, drug addiction, relationships or bereavement.

5. **Rewards and restraints** Both can be very fulfilling but exhausting. Practitioners learn through training how to cope effectively with a full day of other people's miseries. A few – 'agony aunts' (and an uncle or two) – combine the work with

journalism, and become well-known through the press and media.

6. **Useful information**
British Association of Psychotherapists, 121 Hendon Lane, London N3 3PR.

British Association for Counselling, 1 Regent Place, Rugby, Warwickshire CV21 2PJ.

Relate (National Marriage Council), Little Church Street, Rugby, Warwickshire CV21 3AP.

INSTRUCTIONAL

(See also Bridge Teaching, Chapter 4).

Tutoring

1. **Is this for you?** Many teachers take on private students alongside other employment, then turn to tutoring as an alternative career after retirement. There are numerous subjects you could offer: Teaching English as a Foreign Language (TEFL) for adults as well as children; any school-based subject, especially GCSEs or A levels; Common Entrance examination preparation; special coaching for those with learning difficulties. Consider, also, teaching non-academic subjects, public speaking, etiquette, crafts, technical skills etc. Think about the pupils you could teach – ethnic groups, women, executives – and where – colleges, clubs, department stores. The possibilities are endless!

2. **Particularly suitable for** Ideal for qualified teachers with schoolroom experience or anyone with expertise, enthusiasm and communication skills.

3. **Training** TEFL qualifications available from Royal Society

86

of Arts. *Craft work:* exhibitions experience is useful. *Sports:* diplomas/certificates recommended.

4. **Market possibilities** Recommendation from satisfied pupils (or their parents) is best. Start with a few pupils, perhaps via local schools and colleges. Intensive coaching schools sometimes require extra GCSE tutors. Late afternoon and evening work is commonplace for all fields. Non-academic markets include adult residential colleges and education centres. Fee based pay: medium. Language courses for business people tend to be better paid.

5. **Rewards and restraints** One-to-one work is very different from classroom teaching and is best for those who are well organised, confident and professional. Home-based work is possible, but, as tutoring often takes place in pupils' homes, travel is more usual. Tutors say their biggest difficulties come from over-ambitious parents; the good news is that some tutors become very close to pupils and their families, so invitations abroad can be a useful spin-off! Non-academic and adult pupils are self-motivated and are usually a pleasure to instruct.

6. **Useful information**
Department of Education & Science (DES), Sanctuary Buildings, Great Smith Street, London SW1P 3BT.

Incorporated Association of Tutors, 27 Radburn Court, Dunstable, Bedfordshire LU6 1HW.

TEFL, Royal Society of Arts, Westwood Way, Coventry CN4 8HS.

Other possibilities
Consider giving your expertise to groups such as ex-offenders, many of whom have poor levels of basic skills and education. Contact the National Association for the Care and Resettlement of Offenders, Head Office, 169 Clapham Road, London SW9 0PU.

HOUSEKEEPING

Domestic bursar

(See also Chapter 4, housesitting)

1. **Is this for you?** Job titles vary these days for those who supervise domestic services. They may be called domestic service managers or similar, but, for the most part, house-keepers keep house. They work in a variety of establishments, such as hotels, hospitals, schools, residential homes and student hostels; they may be employed by companies with business hospitality accommodation or by individuals who maintain upmarket residences. Their work includes arranging, supervising and inspecting domestic cleaners, checking stores and equipment, paperwork (accounts, for example) and dealing with master keys, maintenance problems, storage, lost property etc.

2. **Particularly suitable for** Anyone with previous domestic experience, although there is a considerable difference in scale between looking after a family and becoming, for example, a hotel housekeeper.

3. **Training** In-house training is often offered by large hotel groups. Contact the Hotel and Catering Training Company for part-time courses. NHS has a training scheme.

4. **Market possibilities** As travel and tourism grows, job availability is good within the hotel and catering industry. Pay: low/medium, but sometimes includes accommodation and board. Income is higher in private and company work.

5. **Rewards and restraints** Good opportunities exist for the older worker who is a meticulous organiser, able to cope in a crisis and able to command respect from both employers and employees. If foreign domestic workers lack English, it is useful to have a smattering of a foreign language; younger staff from abroad sometimes need 'mothering', as do boarding school children. Not for those with tender feet.

6. Useful information
Hotel and Catering Training Company, International
House, High Street, London W5 5DB.

Catering

1. Is this for you? Catering covers a vast range of occupations,
from sandwiches, school dinners, pub/inn ownership, directors' lunches, restaurant meals, weddings, bed and breakfast
and so on. The range is enormous. Look at your time availability, purchasing power, storage space, kitchen equipment
and preparation facilities before deciding to start any
catering operation. All sorts of rules and regulations exist
where food is concerned and must be followed. Always
consult your environmental health officer before starting
anything home-based. Publicans must be licensed personally
by the local magistrates every year and have to comply with
government regulations. Bed and breakfast establishments
need to register for a food hygiene certificate. Chefs and
cooks not only prepare food but also deal with orders, budget
and keep accounts.

2. Particularly suitable for   People with an eye for colour and
imagination make good chefs; B&B providers should like
people (even if they are late and grubby); pub/inn/café
owners need business experience. Restaurateurs come from
all sorts of backgrounds; the ones who stay in business tend
to be hard-nosed business folk.

3. Training   Adults can train as chefs/cooks by taking City and
Guilds certificates. Contact the Hotel and Catering Training
Company for courses on pubs, hotels, restaurants etc. Pri-
vate cookery schools are also available.

4. Market possibilities   Study the market for home-based
services and do not be afraid to try something new: one
woman started up a successful 'Fill Your Freezer' service for
new mums, which expanded to provide for older people
living alone. Offer attractive cuisine for boardroom meals

(fat-free, cold buffet, school puddings). Catering, as a whole, welcomes older adults. Many part-time jobs available, some in split shifts. Variable income.

5. **Rewards and restraints**   All jobs in kitchens require fitness and stamina; publicans and restaurateurs keep long hours – they need an outgoing personality, tireless feet and, so it is said, strong livers. Taking on a 15th-century inn may appear wonderful at first, until you discover the historic plumbing and electrics. Dealing with temperamental staff in hot kitchens can be tricky; dealing with quarrelling couples in the middle of the night may be even trickier. First aid know-how is recommended. Some caterers specialise: providing wedding cakes, for example, or children's party fare. A sense of humour in this work is essential.

6. **Useful information**
The Hotel and Catering Training Company,
International House, High Street, Ealing, London W5 5DB.

The Brewers Society, 42 Portman Square, London W1H 0BB.

Read *The Caterer, Publican.*

CAREER AND EMPLOYMENT AGENCY WORK

Careers adviser

1. **Is this for you?** Although most schools and higher education institutions offer career advice to their recent graduates and present-day students, many other people – especially adults – also look for help when faced with an occupational decision. They may turn to a fee-paying careers service. Independent advisers offer tests and questionnaires to link an individual's aptitudes, interests and personality to different employment fields. Some services go further and

offer a network of job contacts. Maturity is an asset for careers advisers. They know about the practicalities of job-hunting, people and their own careers. In theory, you do not need any formal qualifications to advise anyone about any career. In practice, qualifications are helpful. If you get on well with all kinds of people, can understand and organise complex information, are persuasive, sensitive to others and imaginative, then this is very worthwhile work.

2. **Particularly suitable for** Those with a background in human resources, personnel, teaching, social work, recruitment, outplacement, psychology and counselling.

3. **Training** Available at many levels: postgraduate courses in occupational psychology; diploma courses run by the Institute of Careers Officers and local training boards; in-house training plus workshops from test providers. Over 25s with 5+ years' relevant experience are exempt from many entry requirements.

4. **Market possibilities** Jobs usually advertised in professional journals; for other vacancies, try local/national newspapers. Some professional bodies and charities employ career advisory staff. You stand a better chance of success if you have something special to offer – experience with disabled people, for example, or even the over 50s! Pay: medium/high, but widely variable.

5. **Rewards and restraints:** Paid jobs are most commonly in town or city centres. Do not offer telephone or postal career services: they rarely work. Keeping up to date with the current employment situation and occupational trends is important in this type of work; so is knowledge about training and education, non-paid or leisure activities. Outplacement counselling for those about to retire or be made redundant is currently an active field.

6. **Useful information**
Institute of Careers Guidance, 27a Lower High Street, Stourbridge, West Midlands DY8 1TA.

Employment agency interviewer/headhunter

1. **Is this for you?** Interviewing people looking for jobs and matching them with vacancies suited to their qualifications, experience, skills and personalities is the focus of these workers. Employers, who are looking for staff, give details of their requirements and it is the employment agency or headhunter who 'sells' applicants to hirers and employers to job-seekers. The level of staff – secretarial or top management – determines one's title. For the most part, employment agencies deal with support staff; headhunters specialise in executives.

2. **Particularly suitable for** Anyone with selling skills. Flair, a good memory, well-developed contacts and some management experience are useful for headhunters. Maturity is an advantage in both jobs.

3. **Training** Nothing formal. Many agencies run their own training schemes. Executive selection organisations generally expect consultants to have degrees, but it is not essential.

4. **Market possibilities** These are major city centre-based occupations. There are some recruitment franchised networks, such as The Humana International Group plc. (See Franchising, Chapter 5.) Income: medium–high.

5. **Rewards and restraints** If you can inspire confidence in others, maintain confidentiality, work under pressure and are outgoing and confident, this is an occupation likely to increase in the future and is worth serious consideration.

6. **Useful information**
Federation of Recruitment and Employment Services, 36/38 Mortimer Street, London W1N 7RB.

Institute of Employment Consultants, 6 Guildford Road, Woking, Surrey GU22 7PX.

TRAVEL AND TOURISM

1. **Is this for you?** Tourism is a major UK industry, and work opportunities exist both at home and abroad. The holiday industry has concentrated largely on young employees until recently, but with a fast-growing older population, opportunities for work may be increasing. Tourist information officers are employed by national or regional boards, providing information to visitors and overseeing local hotels, transport and travel organisations. Travel agency staff sell tickets and package trips. Tourist guides usually work in places or towns of interests. Couriers look after holidaymakers, sometimes in holiday destinations or accompanying groups to and from resorts in the UK and overseas.

2. **Particularly suitable for** People who like other people! Good linguists, good listeners, good organisers; competent administrators/secretaries; sales experience, some financial know-how. (Nursing is useful for couriers.)

3. **Training** Essential for travel agents; even if you have previous experience in the field, you will need to update your knowledge of the computer systems. UK tourist guides have a 'Blue Badge' scheme, qualification takes around six months. City and Guilds Certificate courses are available for couriers either at colleges, distance learning (contact ABTA) or individual operators.

4. **Market possibilities** Older applicants' prospects improve with some specialist knowledge or language (Japanese, for example). Some age limits exist in ABTA training. Tourist guides should try information offices in towns and cities. Look for local/national tourist boards, nearby stately homes, historic houses associations; also cruise ships; crafts, sports and leisure interests groups. Mainly freelance work. Pay: low/medium.

5. **Rewards and restraints** There are seasonal variations in this work, although business travel is all year round. Looking

after a group of tourists means working flat out for the length of the tour without time off. You need to be unflappable, a mixture of nanny-cum-head teacher to deal with groups going in and out of coaches, loos, monuments and hotels. Plus points include opportunities to mix with all sorts of people; opportunities to travel to exotic places; some business 'perks' – so it is rumoured.

6. **Useful information**
London Tourist Board, 47 Red Lion Street,
London WC1R 4PF.

ABTA National Training Board, Waterloo House,
11–17 Chertsey Road, Woking, Surrey GU21 5AL.

Institute of Travel and Tourism, 113 Victoria Street,
St Albans, Herts AL1 3TJ.

PERSONAL CARE

Hairdressing

1. **Is this for you?** With the increase in people of both sexes wanting to look youthful, hairdressers are no longer merely technicians but scientists as well. Perming, cutting, styling, bleaching, trimming and colouring are highly skilled procedures these days, so make sure you obtain excellent training. As unisex salons are commonplace, most hairdressers have to deal with a wide range of client needs from short-back-and-sides to long, flowing tresses. Wig making is another branch of the trade.

2. **Particularly suitable for** Warm, friendly people, unflappable and patient, smartly turned out, and with an eye for colour and shape.

3. **Training** Apprenticeships in salons and private courses. Full-time training is available, with some places reserved for

mature students. City and Guilds qualifications. For wig making, see beauty therapy courses. No age limit, no entry qualifications.

4. **Market opportunities**   Someone, somewhere always needs a hair cut, whereas more elaborate treatments depend on the fashion business. Opportunities to work freelance, as an employee or salon owner; also work with children, hospital patients and those in residential care.

5. **Rewards and restraints**   At present, anyone can become a hairdresser without any training. The Hairdressing Council has rightly objected to this and maintains a register of suitably qualified persons. This is not a desk-bound job; you will need physical stamina and well-fitting shoes.

6. **Useful information**
The Hairdressing Council, 12 David House, 45 High Street, London SE25 6HJ.

The beauty business

1. **Is this for you?**   This is a very wide-ranging field. Beauty consultants are employed by cosmetic firms to demonstrate and sell their products. Cosmetic or remedial beauty therapists hide birth marks, disfigurements or blemishes following accidents or plastic surgery. Manicurists are within the beauty business, so are masseurs, beauticians (skin care specialists), pedicurists (feet) and electrolysists.

2. **Particularly suitable for**   Calm, cheerful, outgoing individuals with an attractive, well-groomed appearance. Your own manner must inspire confidence in clients.

3. **Training**   It is advisable although not absolutely necessary. Consult local authority colleges, private schools and cosmetics firms.

4. **Market opportunities**   Maturity is an advantage with some cosmetic houses and salons. A few openings exist in TV companies, modelling agencies, theatres and cruise ships.

5. **Rewards and restraints**   Health and fitness are important here in this very adaptable career. If you have a foreign language, you can work in the business all over the world. As the population ages, there should be more and more work with and for older adults.

6. **Useful information**
   City and Guilds of London Institute, 46 Britannia Street, London WC1X 9RG.

   The International Health and Beauty Council, PO Box 36, Arundel, West Sussex BN18 0SW.

NERVES OF STEEL!

Undertaking/embalming

1. **Is this for you?**   If you are one of those wonderful people to whom others turn in times of distress, you could consider funeral work. Undertakers supervise all funeral arrangements, from the notification of a death to burial or cremation and their work includes preparing a body for its coffin (embalming), paperwork (death certificates, newspaper announcements) and transportation. Embalming may be carried out by funeral directors, but is also a separate occupation. The embalming process preserves and restores appearance to dead bodies and prevents health risks to the living.

2. **Particularly suitable for**   Undertakers need tact, understanding, dignity and good communication skills. Embalming is not for the squeamish, but well worth considering if you can take a scientific, but sympathetic, approach to the deceased and their mourners. Ideal for retired ministers of religion.

3. **Training**   Nothing formal, mostly on-the-job training. A driving licence is desirable. Contact the National Association

of Funeral Directors and the British Institute of Embalmers for recommended qualifying courses.

4. **Market possibilities**   Favourable opportunities for mature adults. Age is an advantage, mature appearance and attitude are assets. Pay: low/medium.

5. **Rewards and restraints**   Many undertaking firms are family businesses which may limit outsiders' opportunities. Newcomers tend to start as drivers, and progress into administration and management later on, but older workers may be able to bypass all this by offering their services as bereavement counsellors, clerical workers and organisers.

6. **Useful information**
National Association of Funeral Directors,
618 Warwick Road, Solihull, West Midlands B91 1AA.

British Institute of Embalmers, 21c Station Road,
Knowle, Solihull, West Midlands B93 0HL.

Driving instructor

1. **Is this for you?**   If you do not mind working unsociable hours and are not inclined to panic, why not become a driving instructor? Thousands of people learn how to handle vehicles every year and many of them are taught – at least part of the time – by an Approved Driving Instructor registered with the Driving Standards Authority. Instructors sit beside the pupil in the car, and give practical lessons and coaching for their driving test. Heavy goods and public service vehicle tuition employs different techniques.

2. **Particularly suitable for**   Patient, even-tempered, above-average drivers who have held a (clean) driving licence for at least four years. Good communications skills with all ages and stages; reassuring and encouraging manner. The Driving Standards Authority requires instructors to be a 'fit and proper person'.

3. **Training**   No academic qualifications. Qualifying examination includes written paper, practical driving and teaching

ability tests. Courses run by specialist training establishments, driving schools; some distance learning available. Trainee licence scheme permits work during training.

4. **Market possibilities** A mixture of opportunities including self-employment, franchise (see Chapter 5) and work for 'multi-car' driving schools. Pupils are mainly youngsters. Pay: medium.

5. **Rewards and restraints** Driving tests are set to change soon to comply with European tests and, as a result, more use may be made of classwork, printed and visual learning material. Watch your insurance rates for this work. It is useful to know about car maintenance and vehicle mechanics.

6. **Useful information**
Driving Instructors Association, Safety House, Beddington Farm Road, Croydon CR0 3XZ.

A VOCATION?

Religious ministry

1. **Is this for you?** All denominations welcome mature candidates as ordained ministers and lay workers. Traditionally, duties include holding services, preaching, conducting marriages and funerals. Nowadays, the work involves a large amount of pastoral care, helping individuals with their personal and spiritual difficulties. Many play a large social role in communities.

2. **Particularly suitable for** Those with a sense of vocation and commitment, plus self-discipline and stamina.

3. **Training** Some faiths require relevant university degrees, but it all depends on the religion in question – most allow shortened training for older adults. No entry requirements

for lay workers; teacher training for some religious school workers. Grants may be available.

4. **Market possibilities**   There are on-going opportunities for work: in inner cities, schools and the military; with young people, prison inmates and hospital patients.

5. **Rewards and restraints**   When you are highly visible and everyone else depends on you, all day, every day, you need plenty of mental stability, physical good health and a strong conviction of your calling. Selection and training is, quite correctly, rigorous.

6. **Useful information**   The best advice for those contemplating the work is to talk with your own minister or rabbi.

The Multi-Faith Centre, Harborne Hall,
Old Church Road, Harborne, Birmingham B17 0BD.

USEFUL ORGANISATIONS

Age Works, ECCO Employment Agency, 3rd Floor, Bedford House, 69–79 Fulham High Street, London SW6 3JW.

Buretire (Bureau for the Retired), Head Office, Willthorpe, High Street, Stanstead Abbots, Herts SG12 8AS (also Bishops Stortford, Cambridge, Letchworth, Waltham Cross and Walthamstow).

Commissioned Officers who are under 60 may find work through **Officers Association**, Employment Department, 48 Pall Mall, London SW1Y 5JY (linked to the Forces Resettlement Service).

Ex-servicemen and women, police, prison officers, firemen, coast guards and merchant seamen: jobs in general management and administration, security, ushers etc. Top age is 60 for permanent jobs; 70 years for temporary work. Not an employment agency, but a membership association, is: **Corps of Commissionaires Management Ltd**, 85 Cowcross Street, London EC1M 6BP.

Do not forget your local **Job Centre**.

Hospice Work: There is *paid* work available in hospices and similar organisations caring for patients with terminal illnesses. The work only offers low/medium pay, but gives huge satisfaction. Contact: Help The Hospices, 34–44 Britannia Street, London WC1X 9JG.

Manpower PLC, 66 Chiltern Street, London W1M 1PR have 150 offices nationwide.

Members of the Institute of Directors, in conjunction with Pauline Hyde & Associates, provide a range of information and advisory services, including career counselling, job search, positive retirement, outplacement assistance. IOD, 116 Pall Mall, London SW1Y 5ED.

NACRO has more paid jobs available than voluntary posts: National Association for the Care and Resettlement of Offenders, Head Office, 169 Clapham Road, London SW9 0PU.

Non-members of the Institute of Personnel Management can use many of their library information services, including a telephone service for UK salary data and training courses, printouts from the personnel management data base and library visits. Invaluable for company research. Fees charged. Institute of Personnel Management, IPM House, Camp Road, Wimbledon, London SW19 4UX.

Part-time Careers Ltd, 10 Golden Square, London W1R 3AF.

REACH (Retired Executives Action Clearing House), 89 Southwark Street, London SE1 0HD.

Royal British Legion, Attendants Co. Ltd, Head Office, 2A Rathmore Road, London SE7 7QW (also Cambridge, Cardiff, Leeds, London, Preston and Poole) provides employment for disabled ex-service people.

Save the Children Fund has a range of paid work available.

Success After Sixty, 307 High Holborn, London WC1V 7UR, an employment agency for people over 50.

Third Age Challenge, established by ReAction and the Community Council for Wiltshire, was formed recently in order to establish re-employment (counselling, retraining, job-seeking new direction courses and, eventually, interim management) initiatives around the UK for the over-50s. A number of groups are already in operation in England, and plans are well in hand for Scotland. Enquiries to: ReAction Trust, St James's Walk, Clerkenwell Green, London EC1R 0BE.

4

Fee and Gift Work

THE FIRST PART OF THIS CHAPTER is devoted to fee work – namely, income derived from results achieved (the second of Charles Handy's work portfolio categories). Following fee work, you will find details of gift work, which is work done for free outside the home.

FEE WORK

There is a vast range of occupations for which fees are paid. Some of the ideas below will be new to you, while others are well known. All have the potential to provide income, interest and satisfaction.

This is not a comprehensive directory of all fee work. It is intended to whet your appetite and offer an overview of just some of the enormous range of freelance occupations.

If you intend to rely on fee work as a major source of income, you are strongly advised to read all of Chapter 5.

Animal Aunt
(see also Working with Animals, Housesitting)

Here are a wide range of employment opportunities for those who are physically fit, experienced with animals and proficient homemakers. You may take care of a person's home, walk the dog and feed the cat, or take over complete responsibility for boarding kennels or stable yards while owners are on holiday. All kinds of animals are catered for (even tarantulas) and the work is 'hands on', that is, *you* do the cleaning, grooming, exercising and everything else. Very high standards are expected: Animal Aunts are 'professional animal carers' and the aim is to 'leave everything better than we find it'. There are no age limits for this work, which may be part-time or full-time on a self-employment basis, less commission. Ex-farmers are particularly welcome, as are all who genuinely love animals and are prepared to care expertly for them, and their homes and gardens. No pay for partners; occasional opportunities to work abroad.

Useful Information
Gillie McNicol, Animal Aunts, Wydwooch, 45 Fairview Road, Headley Down, Hampshire GU35 8HQ.

Bartender

Serving drinks in pubs, hotels, wine bars or cocktail bars is the main work for bar staff who have to know the full range of stock, and how to pour and mix drinks correctly. Bartenders need to be friendly, outgoing people, smart, cool under pressure, with good memories, and fast mental arithmetic. Physical stamina is important: you will be on your feet for hours, and may need to move heavy barrels and other equipment. Most bar staff work part-time with additional hours possible during busier seasons (Christmas, for example). Training is usually on the job, although some breweries have their own programmes.

Useful information
Hotel and Catering Training Board, International House, High Street, Ealing, London W5 5DB.

Brewers' Society Training Centre, 42 Portman Square, London W1H 0BB.

Bee keeper

Unlike many other types of farming such as fish or cattle, keeping bees requires no special licences, little space and low start-up costs (free, if a swarm arrives uninvited). You must acquire hives and other equipment; these may be available second-hand. Find a sunny and warm site near to a good supply of flowers, but far enough away from the neighbours to avoid complaints. Also required are strong backs (lifting honey in and out of the hives is surprisingly heavy) and a liking for outdoor work regardless of weather. This is a top-up source of income, described as 'very fulfilling for those in early retirement'. Check for allergies first.

Training   Local associations and agricultural colleges.

Useful information
Bee Farmers Association, 22 York Gardens, Clifton, Bristol BS8 4LN.

Bookkeeper

If you enjoy keeping financial records and are not terrified by numbers, consider working as a freelance bookkeeper. Many smaller businesses and people such as consultants and the self-employed welcome the services of someone who can sort out their accounts. You may be asked for a wide range of services: just to sort out a paperwork muddle, get the books ready for the VAT inspector, prepare cash-flow forecasts for the bank manager. Nowadays, a computer and familiarity with the relevant software are essentials – the days of Dickensian pen-and-ink book entries are long gone. Qualifications may not be needed, providing you have the background experience and credibility, such as a good-sized relevant work history in an accounts department. With an expanding European market, it could be advantageous to become familiar with foreign accounting procedures.

Useful information Try local accountants, chambers of commerce, trade associations, community college courses.

Bridge teaching

Bridge is one of the most popular card games of all time. It provides challenge, mental stimulation and friendship. Beginners need someone not only to instruct, but also to guide and encourage them. Bridge teachers work from home or at adult education classes, bridge clubs, community centres, even on cruises. They may earn quite substantial amounts or merely top up their income. Some move into tournament organisation or train tournament directors. Others have created small groups with whom they organise duplicate match play which often leads to the formation of a new bridge club.

Training The English Bridge Union Teachers' Association offers short courses, one-day workshops and residential weekends.

Useful information
English Bridge Union Teachers' Association, Ash Grove, Nairdwood Lane, Prestwood, Great Missenden, Bucks HP16 0QL.

Carer

Mature people are highly valued by elderly persons requiring assistance at home. Carers may be residential, perhaps for several weeks with each client, or employed on a daily basis. Their work is very variable and depends on the client's physical state: the frail may require nursing and personal care; those who are reasonably fit but housebound or immobile need lighter assistance with shopping, cooking and help with dressing (putting on shoes is a common problem). If you are in your 50s or early 60s, are physically fit, perhaps with nursing qualifications, get in touch with one of the many agencies offering services to the elderly. The lighter work is also available to those without nursing qualifications. Useful, but not essential, is previous experience of caring for an aged relative, but it is much more important to be accustomed to running a home and family, practical, sensible and – above all – have a sense of humour. References from those who have known you well for at least five years are acceptable. Salary is usually paid directly to you, without deductions for travel costs, board/lodging or booking fees.

Useful information *Yellow Pages* have lists of local agencies; look under Nursing or Domestic.

Checkout operator

Many of the big supermarkets and stores require polite, pleasant, trustworthy individuals who have a responsible attitude to handling cash and can learn to operate electronic tills correctly. As the trend towards larger, self-service stores increases, the demand for checkout operators has grown. Older workers are increasingly welcome and the hours (usually part-time or split shifts) may fit in well with other commitments. This work is a useful 'stepping-stone' back to the workplace from home responsibilities or longer term unemployment as you will acquire customer skills, up-to-date cash handling know-how, as well as a fresh chance to get yourself and your family accustomed to working once more. No formal qualifications are necessary, although some firms require applicants to pass a simple arithmetic test. Major retail companies offer training.

Childminder/Babysitter/Kids' clubs worker

If you enjoy the company of children, there are increasing demands for providing care for children of all ages. To look after other people's children in your own home you must, by law, be registered with the Social Services Department. Contact them beforehand for details of what is involved, training opportunities and support services. *Childminders* are self-employed and work from their own home. Some take under-fives only, others provide after-school and holiday care. It is important to establish a businesslike approach to the work: agree terms (variable, depending on where you live) and have a written contract with parents before taking on a child. Regular discussions about the child's progress are useful, as are financial records. *Babysitters* usually take on short-term care in the child's own home, for an evening, perhaps, or a weekend. Often, such arrangements are very informal: you may be asked to meet the youngsters first and then be left with full responsibility for them while the parents are miles away. Always obtain a contact telephone number, clarify exactly what your responsibilities are and find out what you are expected to do in an emergency. *Kids' clubs* are places where school-age children can play in a caring setting in the hours before and after school, and during all the holidays. New local schemes are being considered all the time. Contact local development officers, via your local authority, for start-up information and advice.

Training and useful information National Childminding Association, 8 Masons Hill, Bromley, Kent BR2 9EY; British Red Cross has an eight-week Babysitter's Certificate Course; Kids' Club Network, 279–281 Whitechapel Road, London E1 1BY.

Desk-top publisher

For those familiar with computers, this is an appealing skill to learn but, arguably, one of the more difficult from which to earn money until you are highly proficient. Good self-promotion is necessary to find work in what is becoming a fast-growth, but very competitive field. Acquire the best available packages and learn how to operate them very well. Just about anything can be desk-top published: books, magazines, advertising, promotional and specialist publications. Use a high-performance computer and printer (laser is best), plus the necessary software packages. Work experience with a publishing house is helpful; for the creative side, you will benefit from graphics know-how.

Training Available from software manufacturers, local art/adult education colleges.

Useful information Relevant computer magazines and software manufacturers.

DIY

Are you handy around the house or garden? Then maybe you could earn a living from woodwork, painting and decorating or helping with other people's gardens. *Carpenters* are nearly always in demand by private customers, particularly for smaller jobs such as making and putting up shelves, cupboards, wardrobes etc. *Painters/decorators* often gain experience in their own homes, then take on work with friends and neighbours. Some specialists skills are welcome, for example: rag-rolling, stencilling, sponging. *Gardening:* maintaining someone else's garden can involve anything from regular summer time lawn mowing to overall responsibility for garden design. Most customers want someone to tackle boring jobs such as weeding and general tidying up; if you have a dodgy back get someone else to do the heavier tasks. All these jobs require an eye for colour and/or detail, background know-how and some financial ability. Jobs must be costed realistically: always provide a written estimate to be agreed before work commences, and have a clear understanding of how and when payment is to be made. Formal apprenticeships in these trades may take years, but you can polish up home-grown skills by on-the-job training or courses at the local technical college leading to City and Guilds certificates.

Dolls' house maker
(see also **Miniaturist**)

Forget about dolls' houses as toys; many of today's miniature homes are serious, collectors' items worth several thousands of pounds. As one expert dolls' house builder says: 'What was once a cottage trade has now become a sizeable industry'. If you have ever yearned to tackle small-scale carpentry (standard size is 1 inch to 1 foot), this is well worth considering. It is 'hands-on' work, particularly suitable for ex-cabinet makers, furniture restorers, carpenters, designers and model makers.

Training There are few miniature courses around, but full-sized techniques are just as effective. Try Adult Residential

Colleges, local classes. Excellent 'how-to' books available from libraries, specialist shops. Joint a local miniaturists' group.

Useful information   The UK premier showcase is the annual London Dolls' House Festival (LDF). Details from LDF, 25 Priory Road, Kew, Richmond, Surrey TW9 3DQ. The *British Dolls' House Hobby Directory* (£3 + large SAE from LDF address above) contains invaluable lists of craftspeople, specialist shops, fair organisers and publications.

Driving

Driving is popular with those who find themselves out of regular employment and there are several different jobs to chose from. Take care, however, to contact your insurance company well in advance to ensure you have adequate cover. *Car hire companies* engage drivers to collect cars from where renters may have left them and return the vehicles to the company premises. *Limousine chauffeurs* pick up passengers and take them to their destinations, helping with luggage, parcels, pets and so on. These drivers must keep their own cars clean and should be able to carry out minor emergency repairs. *Taxi drivers* must be licensed in the UK. To qualify, trainees must be over 21, have no criminal convictions, provide character references, pass a medical and a tough driving test. In London, they must pass a rigorous 'knowledge' of routes and street names. *Mini-cab drivers* use their own cars, operating through controlling companies acting between cab driver and passengers. Mini-cabs may not ply for hire on the streets; their drivers do not require specialised training at the time of writing, although stricter control in future cannot be ruled out.

Useful information
Department of Transport, 2 Marsham Street, London SW1P 3EB.

Examinations staff

Many examination boards engage external examiners. Some actually mark the papers, while others act as overseers to examination staff. Examination invigilators are also required. This involves supervising people taking examinations to ensure the regulations of the examining bodies are complied with and that those sitting the examinations do not cheat. Contact professional bodies, schools and colleges, local education authorities and examination boards such as:

Associated Examining Board, Stag Hill House,
Guildford GU2 5XT.

Joint Matriculation Board, Manchester M15 6EU.

University of Cambridge Local Examinations Syndicate,
Syndicate Buildings, 1 Hills Road, Cambridge CB1 2EU.

University of Oxford Delegacy of Local Examinations,
Ewert House, Summertown, Oxford OX2 7BZ.

Film extra

You do not need an Equity registration (British Actors Equity Association) card if you want to work only occasionally as a film extra, although you should apply to join if you find there is a demand for your services. Non-members may find work through advertisements in local newspapers, direct contact to companies (see *Yellow Pages* under Film and Video Production Services) or by word of mouth. You do not need drama training as you will be told what to do, what clothes to wear, and how and where to go. Ideal for early birds who enjoy a fun few days doing something completely different.

Graphologist

The study of handwriting has been around for a long time, but only recently has graphology achieved a measure of respectability as a recognised, professional skill. Graphologists attempt to infer an individual's health, potential, temperament and attitudes from their handwriting. Handwriting experts are used in personnel selection, recruitment, career development, team and board suitability. Forensic graphology is a recent development requiring further training. It is suitable for those with an eye for detail and an interest in psychology.

Training Some local adult education centres, British Institute of Graphologists recommended tutors, correspondence courses. Apprenticeship with a qualified graphologist is usual.

Useful Information
British Institute of Graphologists, 4th Floor, Bell Court House, 11 Blomfield Street, London EC2M 7AY.

Housesitting
(see also **Animal aunts**)

Increasingly, householders are reluctant to leave their property unoccupied when they go on holiday, thus the demand for recommended caretakers is on the increase. Housesitting agencies seek responsible and mature homemakers, 40–68 years old, with pleasant telephone manners, no other work commitments and very reliable personal references (past employers or individuals of standing). Looking after someone else's home is a big responsibility. You will be provided with basic guidelines to protect your own, and the house owners' interests (for example, no long-distance telephone calls, no overnight visitors, no parties), while saving your own household costs and gaining an enjoyable change of scene, a small income, even a part-time pet or too. Spouses/partner may accompany homesitters, but there are no extra payments to or expenses for them.

Training None necessary.

Useful information
Homesitters Ltd, Buckland Wharf, Buckland, Aylesbury, Bucks HP22 5LQ.

Indexer

An indexer applies special skills to a wide range of materials: written, audio or visual material; books, periodicals, journals; maps, prints or pictures – anything you can think of requiring organised tables. Indexing is good for clear-thinking people who understand how to look things up, have a good eye for detail and want a very flexible job which can fit in with other interests. Computer indexing (disks etc.) work is new and likely to expand. A first degree, especially in medical, scientific, legal or technical subjects, would be very useful.

Training Open learning programme from the Society of Indexers leading to profession recognition.

Useful information
The Society of Indexers, 16 Green Road, Birchington,
Kent CT7 9JZ.

Ironing

Turn other people's dislikes into your income! Many professional people and busy young mums gladly pay up for someone else to do their ironing. Usually, clients expect you to collect their washed but crumpled clothes and deliver back (folded or on hangers) hand-pressed, smooth garments. The best ironing services offer a 24-hour turn-round. Ensure you understand how different fabrics respond to heat. It takes a while to build up a string of clients, but, once established, they are yours providing you do not scorch their best shirt. Some domestic agencies offer contract work. No qualifications are required. Advertise locally.

Kids' party entertainer

Do you fancy yourself as Billy Buttons, Crinkly the Clown or Magical Mike? Talented, outgoing personalities who like children will find plenty of work entertaining them at birthdays, celebrations and local carnivals. You can offer a complete party package covering games, disco, juggling, magic, Punch-and-Judy, films/videos etc., or take bookings for just an hour or so to do your act, then depart. Start-up costs are low: a glove puppet or two, cassette player, story book, some funny hats, balloons, small prizes and a 'magic' wand. A theme (with a jazzy title) is useful. Begin by advertising in local newsagents' windows; later, your name will be passed on by word of mouth. Most work is at weekends or after school hours. You need access to a telephone with a reliable answering machine, plus transport for your costume(s) and props. Keep up to date with juvenile TV, the pop scene and superstars. Perfect for those who are tolerant of little people, physically fit (under-tens can be exhausting!) and have a sense of humour.

Useful information   Anyone else who has survived it! If you prefer someone else to deal with the administration, several agencies (check *Yellow Pages*) provide such work for a fee.

Law costs draftsman

This work has three main areas: assessing the costs that a solicitor should charge a client; computing detailed bills for Legal Aid (presently in the process of change); and, at the end of a case, preparing costs payable by the losing side to the successful party. Do you have an interest in law, plus an aptitude for accounts? Then, this job, open to men and women, offers interest, variety and challenge. Most professionals start by working in a solicitors' office, perhaps in a support role or as a legal executive and then move into law costs drafting later.

Training   Through the professional association's correspondence course.

Useful information
The Association of Law Costs Draftsmen,
66 Ravensbourne Park Crescent, London SE6 4YP.

Lollipop person

School crossing patrols ensure children are escorted safely across the road at certain locations, usually close to schools or areas of heavy traffic. They are employed by the local council, who designate the place of work. Ideal for men and women who like children, are physically fit and do not mind turning out in all weathers.

Training   On the job; no formal qualifications required.

Useful information   Local Town Hall.

Market researcher

Market research is flexible work, ideal for those with other responsibilities. For interviewing work, contact a company direct (try local business telephone books, *Yellow Pages*, Thomson Directory). Ideally, you should be good with people, enjoy working outdoors (for field interviews), and be free to work some weekends and evenings. If you have been in sales, advertising or marketing, you will be especially welcomed. Telephone interviewing is less common, but may be a useful alternative for the housebound. Market Research Society membership offers insurance, advice, education and information.

Training   By the employer.

Useful information
The Market Research Society, 15 Northborough Street,
London EC1V 0AH.

Mediation

If someone you know has ever been involved in a dispute with an ex-partner over divorce arrangements, you will understand how lengthy, expensive and frustrating a process it can be. Mediation is an out-of-court conciliation service which helps opposing parties make joint decisions, often without recourse to formal legal processes. There are diverse areas of mediation. The most familiar are those similar to Mediation In Divorce (MID) in East Twickenham. MID works with divorcing and separating couples, to reduce bitterness and save unnecesary legal costs about settlements for the future, especially regarding children.

In addition, there are community and neighbourhood conciliation groups, such as the Kingston Friends Workshop Group, a non-profit organisation for conflict and problem management. Mediation looks set to expand if the divorce laws are amended and the proposed family advice centres are created. It may also move into other fields such as school mediation, particularly bullying.

Training Entry is no longer restricted to those with specialist backgrounds, although useful experience includes legal, social work, counselling, teaching, youth work, probation work. Training is available via local groups or the national organisation.

Useful information
The National Association of Family Mediation and Conciliation Services, Shaftesbury Centre, Percy Street, Swindon SN2 2AZ. Local Citizens' Advice Bureaux may also have information.

Miniaturist
(see also **Dolls' house maker**)

As with any regular sized establishment, dolls' houses require top to bottom decoration, and furnishing in appropriate style and scale. Miniaturists are delicate-fingered craftspeople who design, make and sell every imaginable accessory for collectors and amateur enthusiasts. A retired expert keyboard instrument restorer uses up his stock of elderly ivories to make intricate musical keyboards – all reduced to $\frac{1}{12}$ scale. Another started her 'Pocket People' kits in a small way by attending classes. She said: 'It never occurred to me at first that I did not have to fully dress every single doll – instead I could sell the kits for people to make up themselves.' She recommends going to dolls' house fairs, helping on a stall, and paying close attention to quality and price.

Training Miniaturists are very generous with help for beginners, so ask questions, heed advice and join a local group. Occasional courses available at adult residential colleges.

Useful information See **Dolls' house maker**.

Model

'Who, me?', I hear you say. 'A model, at my age?' Fashion modelling is, indeed, a youngsters' field, but there are photographic models of any age, male or female. You need good facial bone structure, grooming and grace. Modelling is very suitable for ex-dancers or once-upon-a-time theatre people. Agencies require a photographic portfolio, from which they select suitable models, arrange assignments and take commission on earnings. You are advised to check an agency's reputation before registering.

Training Commercial modelling schools, London College of Fashion.

Useful information
Modelling Tutor, London College of Fashion,
20 John Princes Street, London W1M 0BJ.

Needleworker

Opportunities for those who are good at sewing may be found in various jobs. You should be able to use a sewing machine, have some experience of measuring and fitting, and able to follow patterns. *Dressmakers* may be employed by fashion houses or theatre, film and TV studios; by large stores undertaking alterations; or self-employed at home making clothes for individual customers. *Curtain makers* work for interior decorators, furnishing stores or personal clients. *Tailors/tailoresses* make suits, uniforms, sportswear etc. to individual measurements. Traditionally, the highest grade needle workers have undertaken years of apprenticeship plus further periods in specialist training – cutting, for example. But formal qualifications may not be necessary, providing you can take accurate measurements, are good at fitting and offer competitive prices. You will be more credible with previous workroom experience. City and Guilds certificates are useful.

116

Novelist

Do you have a tale to tell and intend to write a book . . . some time? My mother constantly complained about my childhood 'scribbling', declaring my letters, diaries and essays a 'waste of time'. If only she had known how useful a way it was to learn how to use words and express my thoughts. Beginners are always advised to write about 'what they know', so here the older adult has an edge. Get writing, now – and keep at it! You'll need self-discipline, persistence, single-mindedness and, above all, strong wrists to tear up all the rejection slips which will come your way before the magic day arrives when you hit the jackpot! Writing opportunities may occur in unexpected places: Colin Archer retired at 54, graduated as a mature student and replied to an advertisement for and gained the (paid) post of Writer-in-Residence at a nearby Hospice. His work involves assisting terminally ill patients and those with long term illness to express themselves in words. Colin describes himself as a 'Wordsmith and Fictionmonger'. He teaches Creative Writing and works with Alzheimer patients and reminiscence groups alongside puppeteers and musicians, bringing arts to the handicapped and disabled. Presently, he is busy with a book.

Training Many courses in creative writing at local adult education centres and adult residential colleges. Take care with courses offering 'formulae' for instant best-sellers. If a manuscript is worth publishing, you do not have to pay for it.

Useful information *The Writers' & Artists' Yearbook* (A & C Black) and *The Writer's Handbook* (Macmillan). Both are annual publications.

Piano tuner

If you have a really accurate ear for musc, lots of patience and an interest in keyboard mechanics, piano tuning offers rewarding work with good potential for the future. You visit private homes, schools, colleges, recording studios, choirs and concert halls, and are very likely to become as important to the piano's owner as the instruments themselves. Some piano tuners also undertake the restoration and repair of older instruments, affected by central heating, damp or neglect. Here, expert training is essential. You will need a workshop, tools and specialised transport. Take heed: pianos are incredibly heavy so *never* attempt to shift an instrument alone.

Training Some learn on the job, but courses are recommended. City and Guilds courses may be available.

Useful information
London College of Furniture, London Guildhall University, 41–47 Commercial Road, London E1 1LA

Piano Tuners' Association, 10 Reculver Road, Herne Bay, Kent CT6 6LD.

Private eye

If you have a law, military, police or security background, consider taking up work as a private investigator. Freelancers cover a range of activities for which lawyers, police and official security may not have the time, inclination or resources. This may include simply delivering affidavits and tracing missing persons or complex industrial espionage. A clean driving licence is required, plus stamina and flexible time commitments. Those in the know suggest good contacts (local police, solicitors, larger investigating firms etc.) are important to provide subcontract work, advice and information. There is little '007'-style work.

Training Useful but not essential with the appropriate background. Correspondence courses available in general security, some legal know-how useful.

Useful information
Institution of Professional Investigators, 31a Wellington Street, St Johns, Blackburn, Lancashire BB1 8AF.

Sign language interpreter

Sign has been described as the bridge between the deaf and hearing worlds. Sign language interpreters are qualified professionals who function in a wide range of settings such as job interviews, training courses, union meetings, summer schools, medical surgeries, legal offices, television programmes and live theatre. Demand for registered interpreters outstrips supply. You need to know British Sign Language (BSL) and have good English skills.

Training Numerous BSL courses nationwide. For interpreter courses, contact the British Deaf Association.

Useful information
The Association of Sign Language Interpreters, 30 Albert Road North, Reigate, Surrey RH2 9EG.

British Deaf Association, 38 Victoria Place, Carlisle CA1 1HU.

Snail farmer

Believe it or not, you need planning permission to become a snail farmer! Starting up, you will need a supply of breeding snails, and a well-heated and insulated building; later you will require a processing unit. Sales to restaurants, hotels and specialist food shops are usually through a snail co-operative. Snails are a popular delicacy in France, hence export potential, but consumption in the UK is growing. Franchises are available (see Chapter 5). Your neighbours are guaranteed not to complain about the noise!

Training and useful information
The Snail Centre, Plas Newydd, 90 Dinerth Road, Colwyn Bay, Clwyd LL28 4YH.

Theatrical make-up

I heard about this work from a chance meeting with a 50-year-old ex-dancer who decided to take up theatrical make-up as a second career. Older people adapt well to this field as they are discreet, reliable and not as concerned as youngsters about becoming a celebrity. Opportunities also exist for work with brides, photographers, advertising agencies and magazines.

Training At some art schools, TV companies, the London College of Fashion and other City and Guilds courses around the country. Private tuition available, but it is expensive.

Useful information
London College of Fashion, 20 John Princes Street, London W1M 0BJ.

Toastmaster/mistress

How would you like to be photographed beside the rich and famous? It is always a possibility if you are a toastmaster! They enjoy varied lifestyles: one day with royalty, statespeople and stars, the next at a simple family celebration. Sociable, punctual people with clear voices, good memories, diplomacy and tact make excellent toastmasters. It is best to have modest drinking habits and be able to listen to nondescript speeches with a rapt expression. Good digestion and/or a supply of antacids recommended. Toastmistresses are novel at present.

Training Privately run courses.

Useful information
Guild of Professional Toastmasters, 12 Little Bornes, Alleyn Park, Dulwich, London SE21 8SE.
School for Toastmasters is at the same address.

Welfare work

When employees retire from a large organisation, they are often invited to join a retirees association, and enjoy a number of social and welfare benefits. Welfare field and regional officers monitor the members of these ex-worker groups to provide support, advice and general help. They make regular visits, sometimes overseeing facilities for the elderly or giving financial information to bereaved partners. Welfare officers will usually be paid for a couple of days weekly, plus travel and subsistence. Many combine it with other part-time jobs, and ages range from early 50s to 70+. These jobs tend to go to loyal employees; a personnel background is helpful.

Training None.

Useful information Organisations with a large workforce.

Working with animals
(see also **Animal aunts**)

Did you ever harbour secret longings, years ago, to become a vet? There is lots of other work you can do now with and for animals. What about starting up a pet ambulance service, working in a pet shelter, animal grooming, pet fostering, pet search (lost and found) services, show judging? If you want to find out more about any of these jobs in detail, ask those already involved about the work, consult your local veterinary practice or write for information to any of the addresses below. Pet fostering services provide temporary care for the pets of elderly people who may not be able to manage them for a while because of illness or other emergency. Show breeding and judging (often pedigree cats and dogs, but also other animals) demands expert knowledge of the breed(s) concerned, plus suitable accommodation for rearing litters, veterinary support and sales know-how. Consult local shows, veterinary surgeons and animal magazines. Commercial animal work (pet shops, kennels or catteries) requires licensing and/or planning permission. Enquire at your local town hall for details.

Training Ideally, you should be patient, very fit, reliable and realistic. Try a week's voluntary work with the local vet or kennels first. Training for many of these areas is 'on the job' with some private tuition available; few require formal qualifications. (NB: The RSPCA Inspectorate has an upper age limit of 40 years.) Stroking a cat's fevered brow is no romantic affair when the moggy is sick or injured – think twice if you cannot

121

stand the sight of blood. Think three times before taking on any animal work if you suffer from allergies.

Useful information
Universities Federation for Animal Welfare, 8 Hamilton Close, South Mimms, Potters Bar, Herts EN6 3QD
(send SAE for excellent leaflet).

RSPCA, Causeway, Horsham, West Sussex RH12 1HG
(or your local branch).

Pet Trade and Industry Association, 103 High Street, Bedford SG18 8PB.

GIFT WORK

Voluntary work, or work done for free outside the home, is an ideal way to maintain your credentials during a career break or career switch, or as a means of contributing to the community when income is less important. Unpaid opportunities exist in practically every field. There is a place for everybody and all skills at every level.

The *Good Retirement Guide* (1992, Kogan Page) suggests that there are four broad categories of voluntary help:

- clerical/administrative (such as typing, stuffing envelopes, answering the telephone, organising committees);

- fund-raising (jumble sales, coffee mornings, flag days, sponsored events etc.);

- committee work (treasurer, secretary and so on);

- direct work with the public (driving, delivering and helping handicapped, elderly, homebound or sick people).

Gift work is invaluable for those unable to take up employment at present – for whatever reason. If you have completed the self-assessment section, you will already know what strengths you have to offer and/or which skills you wish to acquire in future. Return to Chapter 2 if you are unsure. Next, consider the benefits of a volunteer job:

- to sample a new field of work
- to obtain work experience for a CV
- to get free training
- to maintain old and develop new contacts
- to obtain references
- to make worthwhile use of your time
- to keep in touch with the workplace
- to illustrate a positive attitude during non-work periods
- to find out about possible paid jobs in the organisation
- to keep up your morale
- to rebuild your confidence

Information resources for volunteer opportunities

Age Concern, 1268 London Road, London SW16 4EJ provides information on local Age Concern groups.

Association of Retired Persons (ARP) centres are run by volunteers.

Citizens' Advice Bureaux (look in your local telephone directory or Thomsons Guide) can be contacted for information on local groups.

Community Service Volunteers (CVS), 237 Pentonville Road, London N1 9NJ operates the nationwide RSVP (Retired and Senior Volunteer Programme) for over 50s wanting to be involved in local community projects.

Employers' retirement groups – large organisations may have their own groups with local branches.

Local newspapers

Your public (reference) library will carry information on local groups. Also try the following: local branches of the British Red

Cross, Samaritans, etc.; local church, synagogue or similar; local hospital – ask for the volunteer co-ordinator or the hospital 'friends' group.

REACH, 89 Southwark Street, London SE1 0HD – set up over ten years ago to place retired men and women with business or other professional skills in voluntary organisations in Great Britain. Finds part-time, expenses-only jobs.

Volunteer bureaux (look in your local telephone directory or Thomsons Guide) can be found in more than 300 towns. They can point those who wish to give their time in the right direction.

Volunteer Centre UK, 29 Lower King's Road, Berkhampstead, Herts HP4 2AB provides information, runs events and training courses.

If you have a good idea for a project, are proactive and a good organiser, you may like to contact the **New Horizons Trust**, Paramount House, 290–2 Brighton Road, South Croydon, Surrey CR2 6AG. Groups of at least ten people, half of which should be aged over 60, may apply for grants up to £5,000 for schemes to improve local amenities or to fill gaps in existing social services.

Choosing the right type of voluntary work

Here are some questions to ask yourself and any organisation before making a commitment to volunteer work.

- Where is the job – nearby, far away, indoors, outdoors, office, kitchen?
- How long am I committed to the job? Indefinitely, a week, six months, two years?
- Exactly what sort of work is involved?
- Whom will I be working with? Nobody, one other person, a team?
- Are there any training opportunities?
- Are expenses paid? How often? How much? What for?
- What about holidays or if I am unwell?

If you intend to move from unpaid work into paid employment, find out the following.

- What skills will I acquire?
- Will references be provided at the end of my assignment?
- Are there prospects for advancement into paid work?

Special interests

You may have a particular interest, skill or qualification and want to use it with a special group. Here are some ideas for you.

- *Architects, builders, surveyors* Heritage, conservation, arts.
- *Befrienders* Youth, the elderly, AIDS (Buddies), offenders.
- *Business* Chambers of commerce, business in the community, small firms advisory services.
- *Canvassing* Political parties.
- *Counselling* Bereavement, alcoholism, drugs, marriage and family.
- *Creative skills* Community art centres, drama groups.
- *DIY* The elderly, housebound, handicapped people. Residential homes.
- *Driving* Hospitals and hospices, sick children, political parties.
- *Under 5s experts* Toy libraries, hospital play schemes, refuges.
- *Gardening* Residential homes.
- *Holiday organisers* Disadvantaged youngsters, disabled people.
- *Literacy* Offenders, local education reading schemes.
- *Marketing public relations* Everyone who needs to raise money.
- *Retailing* Charity shops.
- *Running a coffee shop* Hospitals, hospices, prisons.
- *Running a library* Speaking books.
- *Sport* Youth clubs, disabled people, coaching.
- *Support* Crime victims, housebound, families in crisis.

- *Writing letters* Hospital patients, residential homes, offenders.
- *Youth* Brownies, Guides, Cubs and Scouts, Sea Cadets.

Public Appointments Unit

The Public Appointments Unit maintains a register of people willing to be considered for public appointments. Public bodies are organisations which assist and advise government ministers and departments in the making or application of their policies. They include nationalised industries, executive and advisory bodies, tribunals and certain public corporations (BBC, British Council).

There are nearly 40,000 public appointments, of which a quarter are appointed or reappointed each year. Most are part-time (one to two days a month) and pay travel and out-of-pocket expenses only. Many appointments involve committee work, so the ability to chair a meeting or contribute to group discussion and decision making is essential. Experience in special sectors is useful – every field from arts and banking to education, environment, retailing and manufacturing. Some appointments call for recent senior executive experience, but others are open to people who have retired or have limited recent full-time experience. The qualities required may be acquired through the voluntary sector (arts groups, housing associations, PTA, school governors, for example), as well as full-time work.

You can nominate yourself to be entered on to the register. Nomination forms, available from the Unit, ask you to write a brief 'self-appraisal' of what you feel you would bring to a public appointment by way of experience, interests, skills etc. You can include experience such as bringing up children, experience with a disabled child, or caring for an elderly or disabled person. Two referees are required, plus a current, detailed CV.

Information from
Public Appointments Unit, Cabinet Office,
Horse Guards Road, London SW1P 3AL.

Non-executive directorships

Former senior managers could consider putting their names forward as a non-executive director. Finding high-calibre people to join a board of directors is sometimes a problem for companies. They need the best person for the job, regardless of the names put forward by friends, colleagues, the 'old boy' network and family. If you have the judgement and knowledge of boardroom practice, can defend your point of view, feel energetic enough to work harmoniously with colleagues and have high calibre experience, preferably with a quoted public limited company (plc) contact the following:

- **PRONED**, 1 Kingsway, London WC2B 6XF. Promotion of Non-executive Directors maintains a register of candidates for companies of all sizes.

- **Institute of Directors**, 116 Pall Mall, London SW1Y 5ED. The IOD runs a board appointments service, for use of which membership of the IOD is not required.

Overseas opportunities

Here are some questions to ask yourself and the organisation before committing yourself to an *overseas assignment*.

- What expenses are met by the organisation?
- Do you need to be able to drive? Can you?
- Is transport provided?
- Do you know something about vehicle maintenance?
- Can you type or bookkeep?
- Are you fit and in good health? Is there a medical examination?
- Have you practical skills – cooking, simple DIY, first aid?
- Can you teach or instruct – English, maths, anything?
- How does your partner/spouse feel about going overseas?
- What about your home while you are away?
- Is a resettlement grant paid when the tour of duty is complete?
- Are National Insurance contributions provided (if relevant)?

- Is health/sickness insurance provided for you/your partner?
- Are languages required or training provided?
- Are pre-departure orientation courses and briefings available?
- Is a work permit required – if so, who obtains it?
- Who is responsible for any UK tax liability?
- What about banking arrangements?

British Executive Service Overseas (BESO)

BESO, founded in 1972, is an independent charity which works to transfer skills and knowledge to emerging economies by providing hands-on training and advice. Any public or private sector organisation abroad in need of assistance can request assistance from BESO. An appropriate qualified professional, technical and consultancy volunteer adviser is identified from BESO's register of experts and sent on short-term assignments (two weeks to six months). BESO maintains a register of volunteers with many levels of expertise – chefs and butchers are as much in demand as financial administrators.

BESO pays for travel and insurance; the client provides suitable accommodation, subsistence, and local transport and expenses during the assignment. Spouses may accompany volunteers on all but short assignments. BESO volunteers do not receive pay.

Programmes of assistance have been launched world-wide, including Eastern Europe, Caribbean, Indian sub-continent, Pacific Basin and the Far East. BESO does not guarantee assignments for all volunteers since much depends on what needs are required by clients. A vast spectrum of volunteers is requested, so shortages may occur in certain fields. Recent shortages included those with expertise about plastics, furniture, shoe making, textiles, meat products, paints and varnishes, chemicals, concrete and motor components.

Potential volunteers should contact BESO directly. Complete the registration form as fully as possible, including extra pages, so that all experience – however secondary it may seem to you – is incorporated. Attach a photograph of yourself to the completed application form. Also, give the name and address of an alternative contact in case BESO wants to contact you when you are away from home. If there are special circumstances which could affect your availability for overseas assignments, you should advise BESO. BESO is keen to welcome more women volunteers to assist with the requirements of women in development.

Information from
British Executive Service Overseas,
164 Vauxhall Bridge Road, London SW1V 2RB.

Voluntary Service Overseas (VSO)

VSO is the largest organisation for two-year minimum volunteer opportunities in Africa, Asia, Far East, Pacific and Caribbean. Travel plus living expenses paid, couples welcome (no children) if both have necessary skills. VSO is interested in applicants up to 70 years, with expertise in education, health, technical trades, agriculture, social, community and business development.

Information from
VSO, 317 Putney Bridge Road, Putney, London SW15 2PN.

United Nations Volunteers (UNV)

UNV has specialists and field workers in 115 countries: Africa, Asia-Pacific, Latin America-Caribbean. The main activity is to programme, deliver and administer suitable personnel for technical co-operation and humanitarian work in developing countries. Retired people are very welcome, preferably with academic or equivalent technical qualifications, although lengthy work experience may be substituted. Travel and accommodation provided plus monthly allowance.

Information from
UNV, Palais des Nations, 1211 Geneva 10, Switzerland.

Useful publication

Volunteer Work – the complete international guide to medium and long-term voluntary service contains invaluable information, advice and encouragement sections on all aspects of volunteering in 130 countries, for assignments lasting 3 to 36 months, ages 16 to 70+. Includes short-term work, UK advisory bodies and professional recruitment. Published by the Central Bureau for Educational Visits and Exchanges, London.

5

Working For Yourself

A GOOD IDEA IS NOT ENOUGH . . .

STARTING UP YOUR OWN BUSINESS is very exciting: you feel full of energy, confidence and optimism. Being your own boss sounds so good! You will make some money, become independent and – maybe – create a future family enterprise . . . nothing is impossible! Working for yourself is a growth business; everyone is doing it. But, like so many things in this life, self-employment brings risks as well as rewards.

There are no guarantees in self-employment. Even the most carefully researched businesses can fail and a large proportion of them are new ventures. Yes, you need a sound idea and the ability to produce the goods or services you wish to provide. But you also require a whole range of additional business skills. There are some important personal decisions to be made, too, before going it alone, such as when to take the plunge and family reactions.

There are advantages in turning to self-employment after the age of 50. American writer Albert Myers points out how many older entrepreneurs have less to lose than younger folk. After all, you have already had successes during your first 50 years, and can take strength from and build upon them. You can cope with change, you possess knowledge, you have developed self-reliance and were most likely to have been brought up with a strong work ethic. In addition, you probably have customer-related skills: high standards of quality and service, courtesy and calmness. These qualities are invaluable in today's 'If-you-can't-see-it-we-haven't-got-it' customer climate. All this points towards starting up on your own.

Not everyone wants to become an entrepreneur or freelance, though. And not everyone who starts up a small business will succeed. How, then, can you avoid today's high hopes turning into tomorrow's nightmare?

The first part of this chapter is designed to give you an indication as to whether you have what it takes to run a business or work alone. There are sections on all the basic steps and choices for self-employment. There are separate headings for Rural Businesses, Women in Self-employment and Making Hobbies and Interests pay. If, after you have finished reading, you decide to proceed further, take advantage of the vast number of resources (many are free) available to 'budding' entrepreneurs indicated in the second part. They offer help, advice, training, contacts – practically everything you may require in order to turn your idea into reality and allow your venture the best chance of success.

IS SELF-EMPLOYMENT FOR YOU?

Before you invest hope, time and money, ask yourself if you have what it takes to be your own boss.

	Yes	No
Are you . . .		
1. In good health?		
2. Dreaming of becoming a millionaire?		
3. Driven to succeed?		
4. Looking for a 9 to 5 job?		

	Yes	No
5. Willing to work weekends?		
6. Setting up on your own as a last resort?		
7. Prepared to do any menial task?		
8. New to the business you wish to start?		
9. Looking for independence and control?		
10. Unfamiliar with business skills?		
11. Self-confident? Resilient? Dedicated?		
12. Vague about your business idea?		
13. Able to make decisions and act upon them directly?		
14. Going into business to stop someone nagging you?		
15. Able to listen to criticism without taking it personally?		
16. Going into business for selfish, 'me' reasons?		
17. Becoming self-employed to avoid job-hunting?		

If you have answered 'Yes' to *all* the above questions, you should reconsider your plans. There are some important areas where you will have to find new answers. If you require further clarification, consult your local Job Centre for business advice counselling. This offers you the opportunity to talk through your plans with an experienced businessperson.

If you have replied 'Yes' to questions 1, 3, 5, 7, 9, 11, 13 and 15, *and* 'no' to questions 2, 4, 6, 8, 10, 12, 14, 16 and 17 you are probably in business already! Most readers will feel reassured to proceed further with a *majority* of correct responses. Take care with the incorrect answers: they indicate some considerations to explore further.

First steps

Most experts suggest that there are several basic steps to be taken before going self-employed. First of all, the decision to go it alone should not be taken on the spur of the moment. Early on, talk with your family, friends and colleagues, and discover if they are prepared to support you. Attend a one-day general introductory course and book a business counselling session. Consult an accountant, solicitor and bank official.

Next, you must have a marketable idea. Whatever you intend to offer, your product or service must fill a market gap and meet a demand. If you want to set up a window cleaning service, find out first if anyone needs a window cleaner (and, if it is for business premises, at what time the work is carried out).

Ask yourself time and again – who are my customers and why should they buy from me? Look at your business idea from a prospective customer's viewpoint – in what ways am I able to offer something better/new/extra/unique/cheaper/simpler? Your business idea, the product or service offered and your intended market must be thoroughly researched prior to start-up.

Thirdly, however beautifully you may decorate wedding cakes, type manuscripts or design jewellery, if you intend to set up an income-producing *business* – as opposed to a pin-money hobby – you must understand the world of business. You will need to know about managing time, finance and people. You have to know about marketing, promotion, bookkeeping, record-keeping, selling and costing. Take stock of your business know-how and obtain help, advice and training to fill in any gaps.

Self-employment

Self-employment means working for yourself. It covers several forms of working conditions, including freelancing and setting up your own business. The main criterion, for tax and National Insurance purposes, appears to be that you are 'working at your own risk', but it all depends on the trade, industry or occupation in question. Obtain professional advice from an accountant before you start.

Freelancing

Freelancing is a very flexible, transferable form of self-employment. As a freelance, you can teach, offer a service, set up as an independent, become a sole practitioner or call yourself 'consultant' in practically anything. Usually, freelancers are trained in employment first, taking after-hours jobs and using work contacts alongside their regular employment until they are ready to set up on their own. Others go freelance as a result of redundancy or retirement, or just because they like the idea of working for themselves.

One of the main problems with freelancing is how to keep up a flow of incoming work. Not only must you be proficient at the service you offer, but you must also maintain your visibility and self-marketing. Employers vary in their attitude to freelance workers. Some see consultants as cost-efficient; others remain sceptical. To increase your chances of success as a freelance, tread a careful line between over-modesty and brashness. You are more likely to gain work if you have excellent, convincing credentials which employers recognise. Avoid presenting wordy lists of vague qualifications, over-elaborate business cards and bundles of press cuttings. Take a course in self-presentation skills, talk to others and read some books *first*.

Options for setting up new businesses

Getting Started – a London Enterprise Agency (LEntA) publication, available from LEntA, 4 Snow Hill, London EC1A 2BS – offers four options for new businesses. These are:

- introducing a new product or service
- developing an existing product or service
- buying an existing business
- buying a franchise

Providing a service These are personal/professional activities based on using your time, skills and equipment for those who cannot or do not want to do the job for themselves. It involves the least risk and smallest capital outlay.

Selling involves buying or producing goods to sell and requires more initial business knowledge, capital and higher risk.

Manufacturing converts raw materials into finished goods. It is the most expensive start-up business needing capital, equipment, premises, know-how and business skills.

Wholesalers are the middle distribution links between manufacturers and retailers.

Retailers sell goods, products and commodities direct to customers.

Mail order sells goods by post or mailing services to customers who have ordered the goods, products or commodities from advertisements, catalogues etc.

Introducing a new product requires specialist advice on patents etc., licensing, funding, technology and marketing.

Buying a business Specialist, professional advice is absolutely essential. Never, ever buy an existing business without first obtaining all the details, finding out if the information is reliable, discussing it with an independent adviser and then sleeping on it. Ask, check, discuss, STOP and think!

Franchising A franchise is where the owners of a business allow others to sell their products or services under their own nationally promoted name. The system has pros and cons. From the business purchaser's viewpoint (the franchisee), gains include training, independence, less capital, bulk purchasing and reduced business risk. But there are controls imposed, quality standards to maintain and initial fees to be paid. The British Franchise Association (address on page 147) offers information packs, professional advisers and members lists. Information is also available from some government departments and high street banks.

Business legal structures

A business may trade as one of the following:

- sole trader

- partnership
- limited company
- co-operative (may also be a partnership or company)

Sole trader status

It is very easy to set up as a sole trader. All you have to do is tell the Inland Revenue. You gain complete authority and control, but have unlimited liability (including the family home and car) for business debts if the business fails. You are liable for personal income tax on all profits and pay Class 2 National Insurance contributions. There are no special registration procedures, but if you do not trade under your own name, you must disclose your name on the business stationery etc. Also, inform the Department of Social Security that the business exists.

Partnerships

This is where two or more people set up in business jointly under a legal agreement. They share the workload, profits and each other's talents. Tax, National Insurance and registration procedures are the same as for sole trader status. Partnerships have unlimited debt liability plus possible liability for partner's debts. Do not leave partnership agreements to chance – consult a solicitor.

Limited company

If your business is a private limited company, it means you will not be responsible for the company debts (unless the company has been trading fraudulently). A limited company used to require at least two shareholders, but since summer 1992, it is possible to set up a limited company with one shareholder only. Solicitors will arrange this for you or you can buy one 'off the shelf' from a registration agent – do not try to do it yourself. Tax is paid on salaries from the company's profits; National Insurance Class I contributions from both employee and the company. Small companies, with turnover less of than £90,000 p.a., are not now required to have their books audited by an independent accountant, but it may be that institutions such as banks may still require audited records for loans, etc. Audit requirements for medium sized companies have also been modifed – full details available in 1994 Finance Act. Take note that companies set up since Autumn 1993 are required to assess their own tax returns. Ask for help and advice from the resources listed under 'Who can Help' at the end of this Chapter.

Co-operatives

These are generally worker controlled and owned in manufacturing and service industries. There are no legal definitions of a workers' co-operative, but there are legal requirements for setting one up. Co-operatives spread the risks and loads; ideally, these should be equally shouldered, but, in practice, imbalance often leads to failure later. If you want to start or join a co-operative, be realistic from the start: think about your objectives, the group characteristics, working relationships, structure and constitution. Take a solicitor's advice or ask for help from one of the resources below.

A very helpful free leaflet, clearly illustrating the necessary steps and differences, is available from the Department of Trade and Industry (see address below). Ask for 'Setting Up in Business – a Guide to Regulatory Requirements'.

Business names

You cannot employ a name already being used by someone else in the same trade or locality. There is no need to register a business name unless it is a limited company, but it is a good idea to make sure. You can register a trade mark or logo. If you are a sole trader or partnership, you must print your business name and address on all business stationery and at the business premises, unless you are trading under you own name. Contact Companies House, Crown Way, Cardiff CF4 3UZ for help and advice; the Department of Trade and Industry (see address on page 135) is also helpful.

A professional approach to small business

There is a vast amount of information available for anyone considering starting-up their own business. Enquire first locally for Small Business Information services. Look in *Second Chances* for details of Training for Self-employment and at Part 2 of *Independent Careers* (edited by Boehm and Lees-Spalding, publisher Bloomsbury) where basic information is spotlighted in the useful section 'How To Go About It A-Z'. Obtain a copy of *Be Your Own Boss* from the Federation of Small Businesses (32 St Annes Road West, Lytham St Annes, Lancashire FY8 1NY) and send off to the Department of Trade and Industry Small Firms Publications, PO Box 1143, London W3 8EQ for free publications including 'Your Guide to Help for Small Firms' (PL889). See also 'Who can Help' at the end of this Chapter.

Specialists suggest the following are core essentials for small business start-up:

The business plan

You will need to write a business plan which defines your business objectives and how you expect to achieve them. Special forms are available from your bank, with prompt questions which you should be asking yourself. Enterprise agencies have helpful booklets.

Adequate capital

Outside financial help is often required for a business start-up. Your bank manager may be able to advise you; also consider government start-up schemes. If one bank refuses you, take heart and try another! Not all banks are interested in making business loans. Lenders require most older borrowers to take out insurance against a loan just in case you die before the loan is repaid.

It is very likely that you will be expected to put up some of the finance from your own resources. Do not gamble all your life savings on any one business venture – yours or anyone else's. If you have a redundancy or similar lump sum available, do not invest more than you can afford to lose. Your financial backers will require evidence of creditworthiness. This may include character references, details of your previous relevant experience, the capital *you* are prepared to invest and collateral.

Collateral is a tangible form of security which a bank or other lender could normally expect to use to repay the loan should your venture fail. Very often this is a person's house or savings. Take care that you really understand the consequences of anything you sign over as collateral. In a limited company, it is quite usual for a bank to seek 'directors' guarantees' for loans made to the firm. This means directors are liable to repay from their personal resources loans on which the company has defaulted.

Professional advice

Accountants can advise on matters such as preparing a business plan, business accounts, tax and VAT liability, cash flow and budget forecasting.

Solicitors' help includes employment legislation, legal formation of a limited company, contracts, partnership agreements, patent and copyright law.

Your bank manager can help determine your financial requirements. Some banks have small business advisers and offer free banking to new businesses.

Market research

Consider the following questions.

- Is there a demand for your business?
- Who are your customers?
- Who are your competitors?
- What price will be fair for your product or service?
- Can you make a profit at that price?

If you do not have clear answers to these and similar questions, you need market research. Use trade magazines, directories, competitors' literature and personal enquiries. Telephone similar businesses and ask for their brochure, price lists, samples; look through *Yellow Pages* and Thomson's Directory and compare advertisements. Try a test run: sell a product at a market stall; offer a service at a local community centre.

Advertising

Potential clients or customers need to know that you exist. Visibility, as the jargon calls it, depends on promotion in local or national press, in telephone directories, in leaflets, mailshots or by word of mouth. Editorial features are great! Tell your local newspaper and trade magazine about anything interesting or unusual. Some annual publications – directories, diaries etc. – will include your details free.

Running a market stall and weekend trading

Thinking of making some extra money with a market stall or weekend trading at shows and fairs? The idea of a part-time business may well fit in with your plans, as it allows you to stock up, travel, do another job and keep in touch with others. You can sell your own products, merchandise made by others, a service (e.g. face painting, sculptured nails, computerised horoscopes) – the list is endless. Practise first at local events which charge low or no entry fees – church and school fêtes, private charity events.

Once sufficiently confident, find exhibiting opportunities via your local chamber of commerce, arts centre, exhibition hall, newspapers and craft/trade journals. Book early! Many craft fair operators distribute flyers advertising future events. Fees vary. Usually provided are a 6ft × 3ft trestle table, background screening and a chair (two, if you are lucky!). Bring your own display stand(s), table covering(s) – large, coloured bedsheets are good here – lighting, plus your goods for sale, receipt book, wrappings and small change. Lighting extension plugs are nearly always needed. Include a selection of useful tools – screwdriver, scissors, drawing pins, sticky tape and so on. Wear comfortable shoes and use a money belt. Mark all your goods with a clear price tag; keep small or valuable items under glass or similar. Arrive early, expect to pack up and go home late – most fairs expect exhibits to remain intact until the last customer leaves.

If your display remains *in situ* overnight, consider insurance. Take a friend along with you to act as an extra pair of hands and eyes, and as a stand-in when the booth is unattended. There are some unwritten rules of etiquette which newcomers may like to know, such as not smoking or eating on your stand, never running down other vendors, keeping quiet and being polite to everyone, leaving pets and children at home and – above all – keeping to your allotted space.

Useful books include *How To Be a Weekend Entrepreneur – Making money at craft fairs and trade shows* by Susan Ratcliff (1991, $9.95 + p&p from Marketing Methods Press, 1413 E. Marshall Avenue, Phoenix, AZ 85014, USA, Visa and Mastercard accepted) and *Running Your Own Market Stall* by Dave J. Hardwick (1992, Kogan Page).

Car boot sales/garage sales

Until recently, car boot sales and garage sales were used mainly for householders to dispose of items which they no longer required. Some continue to offer personal bits and bobs, but others, particularly car boot sales, have become more commercialised as increasing numbers of regular traders use these events as inexpensive outlets for their goods and services. A word of caution though: keep a careful eye on the legal or tax position of these and similar types of sales as they may attract the attention of the Inland Revenue, especially if on a regular basis.

Car boot sales are outdoor events, so wrap up well. Look in your local newspaper for forthcoming events; try to visit one or two before setting up on your own, since some car boot sales have a better attendance than others. Arrive early (6 a.m. is not uncommon!) to ensure a good pitch. Do not expect to make a fortune – hard bargaining and haggling is the order of the day. Keep your eyes wide open for the light-fingered brigade and watch out for those little darlings with toffees or ice-creams. As with market stalls, price everything clearly, use money belts and have a co-worker.

Garage sales require similar attention and assistance. Advertise the event in a local paper, shop windows and notices on your gatepost. Label everything with a clear price tag and arrange items sensibly: place all breakables securely, preferably on a separate display. You do not want someone reaching over china or glass to browse through a paperback book. Clear out everything you do not wish to sell from the garage. Do not allow anyone into your house and keep out-of-bounds areas firmly locked. If a purchaser wants to return later to collect goods – a large item, perhaps – make sure you have someone else around at the time.

Rural businesses

Individuals living in rural areas of England already running or thinking of setting up a business can obtain technical advice, training, management, marketing and sales promotion help from the Rural Development Commission. Specialist advice (setting up a village shop, for example) and training in traditional rural skills is also offered; some loan assistance, too. Contact the Business Adviser at the Rural Development Commission, 141 Castle Street, Salisbury, Wiltshire SP1 3TP. For Scotland, Wales and Northern Ireland, separate bodies exist. Enquire at your local Job or Advice Centre, public library or town hall.

Women in self-employment

The advantages and disadvantages of self-employment apply to both men and women of all ages, so please read all the preceding information carefully. Women, especially returners, often think of running a business from home as a first step back to the workplace. Many have already sold their time, produce or expertise on a mini-basis, while bringing up a family. But, women over 50, possibly accustomed to traditional marriages, may not have had a money-earning career until a change –

143

empty nest, spouse unemployment, divorce etc. – sent them out to find paid work. In these circumstances self-employment is a useful alternative to a salaried job.

Below are listed the factors with which women may need special help when planning to work for themselves.

1. **Self-confidence** This can involve anything from worrying about the family to coping with a very successful enterprise. Returners, particularly, may find it worthwhile to join one of the many training courses, support groups and networks available nation-wide. The Women Returner's Network publishes an annual directory of education and training for women which is packed full of information for returners of all ages and stages. *Contact:* The Women Returner's Network, 8 John Adam Street, London WC2N 6EZ.

2. **A good idea but nothing else** *Read* the paragraphs above!

3. **Approaching a bank** Bank managers often seem, probably quite unintentionally, to represent insurmountable bastions of traditional, male chauvinism and thus terrify women seeking business finance. If you start small, your finance needs will probably be small and that is probably best for many start-up women. But, if you have a really good idea, start borrowing. Take the mystery out of bank negotiations by thorough preparation and planning. Be sure of your facts; design a short presentation, briefly stating what your business is about and selecting the best reasons for doing it. Highlight your relevant experience and background. Practise in front of a friend or relative and get them to ask you awkward questions. You need to anticipate any objections with positive, reasoned replies. Stick to factual information – number crunching goes down well. Do not giggle, hang your head or whisper. Leave your party make-up at home and button up. Pay attention to what the bank person has to say and concede any points against your plans graciously. If you present yourself in a businesslike manner, the chances are you will be treated similarly.

Also, read chapter 7 on Interviews.

Making hobbies and interests pay

There is nothing wrong with turning an enjoyable activity into an income supplement, always providing you are aware that only a modest return is likely to result from your endeavours. This does not mean, however, pricing your goods or services at rock-bottom rates. If you do, you are likely to incur the displeasure of others in the field who may be trying to achieve a higher income level.

Here are a few sensible steps which apply to almost every occupation for turning hobbies and spare-time interests into money.

1. Study the existing market carefully. Read everything you can lay your hands on, attend fairs, visit shops, obtain catalogues, local directories etc. to see what, if any, competition exists for your product or service.

2. Ask yourself: why should anyone buy your product/service rather than the others? In what way is it different, better, unique?

3. Have you the facilities and/or the inclination to produce in quantity? It may be fun to create one or two items, but can you cope with several dozen identical ones, week after week?

4. Do you need any special licences, permissions and/or insurances to work from home?

5. Can you divide your life when working from home? Do you need privacy, special equipment, storage space or similar?

6. How will your family/neighbours cope? Will your activity involve noise, visitors, obstruction?

7. Ensure your stock/equipment/tools/products are child-proof and pet-proof, secure and unlikely to cause hazards.

8. Cost your product/service realistically. Take account of your time and materials, keeping in line with similar commodities.

9. Take financial advice from the professionals and stick to it.

10. If appropriate photograph all your finished work, because, once sold, you can no longer show it to prospective buyers.

11. You will need business cards, brochures and price list(s). It may be appropriate to charge for a brochure with photographs.

12. Approach associations/guilds etc. for assistance, support and membership to enhance your credibility. An example is the Embroiderers' Guild, Apartment 41a, Hampton Court Palace, East Molesey, Surrey.

WHO CAN HELP?

Banks High Street banks all display leaflets offering brief advice. Some publish booklets about starting your own business; others publish a series, such as Barclays Guides, to help your business once it is up and running. Generally speaking, you should do your groundwork, especially market research, before making an appointment to talk finance with the bank manager.

Adult education classes Your local community college may have courses. Look in their brochures under Business or Management Studies, and/or Starting Your Own Business, Getting Started in Business, Business Skills for Mature Students etc.

Books There are numerous self-help publications available for all aspects of self-employment. Your public library is a good starting point; look under: Small Business; Business Basics; Working for Yourself; and Running Your Own. . .

Business schools around the UK sometimes provide part-time courses.

British Franchise Association, Thames View Newtown Road, Henley on Thames, Oxon RG9 1HG, offers information packs, professional advisers and members' lists.

Colleges   The Professional Development Unit (PDU) at the London College of Printing and Distributive Trades (Elephant and Castle, London SE1 6SB) offers a good example of the range of workshops, seminars and short conferences held by colleges around the country. PDU, above, offer practical help for adults (not students) in guiding people towards full-time employment and have held one-day seminars on franchising and freelancing. Contact your local college to find out what is available there.

Enterprise agencies   These are teams of advisers specifically set up to explore and support viable business ideas. The London Enterprise Agency (LEntA), set up in 1979, is the largest in the UK, providing a comprehensive range of free advice and subsidised training on business planning, marketing, accountancy, innovations, taxation and premises. It is open to both start-up and established businesses. Regional/local enterprise agencies may be found in Thomson's Directory. Loans may be available through an Enterprise Agency, for example, London Enterprise Agency (LEntA), 4 Snow Hill, London EC1A 2BS.

Job Centre, advice centre and library   Ask for nearby sources of general help, business counselling, advice and information at any of the above. In addition, enquire if there is a business advice centre and business library in the neighbourhood.

National Extension College, 118 Brooklands Avenue, Cambridge CB2 2HN offers distance learning business courses.

Open University   The Open Business School offers a Small Business Programme and Women into Management – both are short courses. The Open Business School, Dept 1456, Winterhill, Milton Keynes MK6 1HQ.

OwnBase, 57 Glebe Road, Egham, Surrey TW20 8BU is a network for self-employed people.

Training and Enterprise Councils (TECs) are responsible for helping unemployed people train for self-employment. TECs are companies run by business and community leaders to meet local needs. Although there are variations, most provide enterprise training and allowance schemes. Consult your local Job Centre, bank or telephone book.

Trade associations, chambers of commerce, professional directories   Details of these should be locally available.

6

Opening Doors

DID YOU LEAVE SCHOOL at 14 or 15 without any qualifications whatsoever? Did you go immediately into work as an apprentice, office junior, pool typist, articled clerk, probationer, raw recruit, trainee? If so, you are not alone. Many of today's over 50s had no choice about the age at which schooling ceased or their lack of paper credentials.

Up to 1944, the State education system allowed only a minority of children the opportunity to sit examinations. Changes after the Second World War, when jobs depended much more on education, required pupils to take an examination at the end of their primary schooling – the infamous '11-plus'. These results decided their entry into one of three secondary systems: grammar, technical or secondary modern school. Although the intention was to provide a system of equal types of schooling geared to the talents of each child, the effect was to limit many youngsters from a very early age. Those who failed their 11-plus examination went to schools which concentrated on technical subjects rather than university entrance or, with secondary modern pupils, to be so non-academic as effectively to prevent them from sitting any public examinations. The youngsters who did manage to obtain school certificate and matriculation, which ended in 1950, were able to go straight into apprenticeships for recognised professions, Now, they need a degree, but this was not so years ago.

Women, who were particularly disadvantaged by the system, were heavily influenced by the social expectations of the day. Girls' education was considered to be a waste of time; after all, they would soon marry and, ideally, be 'kept' by their husbands.

Young women took dead-end, unskilled jobs as stop-gaps between school and marriage or, at best, learned shorthand and typing as something which would 'always be useful' in the unfortunate event of having to earn their own living. How unthinking it was! If only these women had been given the chance to develop their potential earlier, maybe we would not have so many disadvantaged older widows or divorcees now.

Now everything has changed: jobs are no longer for life and qualifications are essential. Lack of qualifications hamper many older adults seeking work. The answer is second-chance education and training. There is such a vast range of educational and training opportunities from which to choose that it is impossible to give a complete guide here. The most comprehensive book on adult education and training opportunities around the UK is *Second Chances* (Careers and Occupational Information Centre); consult the current edition at your public library. In this chapter, the following pages will give you an overview of:

- who needs education and training
- the benefits of education and training
- where you can study
- what you can study
- what to find out before enrolling in a course
- getting started after a long break
- applying to university
- getting the best out of a course
- surviving as a mature student
- finance
- useful help and information

WHO NEEDS EDUCATION AND TRAINING?

Everyone and anyone!

There are no age limits to learning. Do not allow anyone to

persuade you that you are 'too old to learn', or that you cannot remember or concentrate at your age. Psychological research has shown that the ability to learn does not deteriorate with age. Any observable changes have been linked, not to our chronological age, but to different methods of learning at different times of our lives. In other words, older adults do not learn the same way as schoolchildren. This does not mean older people are worse or wrong. It means just what it says: different.

What does frequently happen, however, is that older adults are placed under considerable pressure to behave in a socially permitted way that is thought to be appropriate for their age. As a result, older adults undervalue their potential for learning. I well remember getting subtle disapproval from my own teenagers while I was a student. In their view, 40-something mothers did not spend hours with their noses in textbooks, worring about exams, wearing jeans and college sweatshirts! Do not allow yourself to be dragged down into this type of trap. Everyone, at any age, has the capacity to learn something new – and the mental exercise involved is just as important for your overall well-being as physical exercise.

If you felt a failure at school; if you feel you have spent too long away from studying; if you believe you cannot absorb new information nowadays or fear you will be unwelcome among younger students – think again. School learning was only a tiny part of your life. Everyone over 50 has picked up lots of know-how on the way, so you are probably better equipped to learn than you realise. Learning gets easier as time goes by because you have the experience and the good sense to know what is good for you. Adult learners mix well with other students of all ages and stages. They often surprise their teachers with their strong will to succeed and offer a mature balance to a year's intake of young undergraduates whose views of the world are so much less experienced.

Whatever your situation, age, interests and experience, returning to education and training is a worthwhile investment of your time, energy and potential. Yes, you can teach 'an old dog new tricks'; do not let anyone persuade you otherwise! I know, because I did it!

THE BENEFITS OF EDUCATION AND TRAINING

Let us start by making it clear what is meant by education and training. Education is about learning things that will be of interest to you in your life generally, while training tends to be about learning skills for a job. If you refer back to Chapter 2, you will find that education is similar to those *transferable skills*, while training offers *work-content skills*. Both are enjoyable ways of expanding your mental and creative horizons.

Education and training opens doors. It may not gain you a job, but it certainly gives you a better chance of obtaining an interview. My own psychology degree did not get me my first 40+ job, but it certainly enabled me to pass through the early application hurdles and meet the selection board face-to-face. Courses completed provide evidence on your CV of your perseverance, determination and resourcefulness. They may permit you entry into a particular job, previously denied, or help you pass examinations towards a higher level qualification. They help you update and broaden your skills, develop new ideas and acquire new perspectives on commerce, manufacturing and technology.

Work and employment are not the only doors which may be opened by education and training. The principle of lifelong learning is now generally accepted by individuals and those in authority. Non-vocational education for adults is well recognised as a worthwhile pursuit and even a preventive health measure. Adult classes provide the company of like-minded people, mental stimulation and refreshment, and new experiences. For many, it is a chance to make up for missed opportunities, to satisfy curiosity, to clarify thinking and to stretch the mind. Some learn practical skills such as car maintenance or carpentry; others take up a foreign language or word processing; a craft or sport; an academic subject or diploma course.

The benefits of education and training for adult learners can be simply described: enjoyment!

WHERE CAN YOU STUDY!

Distance learning

The Open University (OU) is for everyone over 18, regardless of age, background or qualifications. Programmes include professional training, postgraduate courses, first degrees, short courses and community education. The 'Studying with the Open University' brochure lists 150 9-month courses which you can take without going for a degree. 'The Leisure Series' is a series of self-contained, multi-media resource packs in subjects such as arts, music, environment, computing and literature, with no set time limits. For degree students, tutor support and study centres exist throughout the UK with short residential schools on some courses. Contact The Open University, PO Box 625, Milton Keynes MK1 1TY.

National Extension College offers over 100 flexible learning courses which you can study when you want, at your own pace and to suit your lifestyle. There are no entry qualifications. You can start any time and have one-to-one tuition. OU preparation courses, GCSEs, A levels, learning skills, languages, business skills, personal development, computer courses, degree, professional and technical training are all offered. Contact National Extension College, 18 Brooklands Avenue, Cambridge CB2 2HN.

The Open College of the Arts was established in 1988 and offers a wide range of art courses. No experience or qualifications are required. Over 50s are encouraged to apply. Courses in art, design, drawing, creative writing, garden design, music, painting, photography, sculpture, textiles, understanding Western art and video production are all available. Tutor support at local centres or by post. Contact The Open College of the Arts, Houndhill, Worsborough, Barnsley S70 6TU.

The Open College concentrates mainly on updating skills and retraining. More than 60 courses are offered, including professional accountancy courses, mostly business oriented. The College has some links to Channel 4. Contact The Open College, Freepost, TK1006, Brentford, Middlesex TW8 8BR.

The Open Learning Foundation is a newer network of former polytechnics and higher education colleges. Contact Open Learning Foundation, 24 Angel Gate, City Road, London EC1V 2RS.

Learning in later life schemes

There may be special provision for the 50+ age group in your area. Ask for information at your local Citizens' Advice Bureau, Educational Guidance Service for Adults (ask for your nearest service at the Job Centre or Careers Service, or look in *Second Chances*; there are 150 of these centres around the country), Workers' Educational Association, Adult Education Centre, or Community College. Age Concern may also be able to help.

Day and evening classes

Usually available through local education authorities. In general, further education colleges offer full-time and part-time courses, mostly towards examinations. Adult education usually provides part-time courses only for adults. You can take up practically anything from accountancy or acrobatics to yachting and yoga, depending on availability. Londoners may obtain *Floodlight*, published annually; others should look for course details in their local library, newspaper, town hall etc.

The Workers' Educational Association (WEA) runs part-time classes, open to anyone, in response to local needs. Contact your branch secretary, address usually obtainable from the local library.

Extra-mural classes These are (mostly) provided by university departments of continuing education. Many courses have no entry requirements or entry tests. Some count towards degrees, diplomas or certificates; other classes are interest based. Courses vary in length and may be found at a variety of centres, so you do not always have to travel to the campus. Contact your local university extra-mural department. For London, contact Birkbeck College, University of London

Centre for Extra-mural Studies, 26 Russell Square, London WC1B 5DQ.

Radio and TV

For information about radio and television courses, contact:

- BBC Education Information, BBC White City, London W12 7TS
- your local ITV franchise group (look in the telephone directory)
- Channel 4, The Editor, Support Services, 60 Charlotte Street, London W1P 2AX
- Channel 4 Clubs, PO Box 4000, Cardiff CF5 2XT

University of the Third Age (U3A)

U3A aims to make education available to older people in local communities by sharing and exchanging views on a wide range of topics. Activities are organised by the members themselves and there are no qualifications or exams involved. Contact U3A, National Office, 1 Stockwell Green, London SW9 0JF for details of a group in your area.

Study Breaks

A pleasant change from regular classes, which includes an opportunity for meeting new people, is a short residential course. This is a popular way of combining a break away from home with instruction. Adult residential courses are listed in the twice-yearly directory *Time to Learn*, available from National Institute of Adult Continuing Education (NIACE), 19b de Montfort Street, Leicester LE1 7GE.

Day and weekend courses are open to all at Oxford and Cambridge. Contact Oxford University Department for Continuing Education, 1 Wellington Square, Oxford OX1 2JA and University of Cambridge Board of Continuing Education, Madingley Hall, Madingley, Cambridge CB3 8AQ.

Summer schools are equally enjoyable. Many independent boarding schools, such as Millfield, Taunton and Marlborough, open their facilities to adults and families during the summer vacation. Oxford University Summer School for Adults takes place during July and August (address above). Obtain a copy of the Summer Schools Supplements from Independent Schools Information Service, 56 Buckingham Gate, London SW1E 6AG, or get in touch with each school direct (consult your library for addresses). Summer Academy is a consortium of universities offering one-week courses during the long summer break. Contact Summer Academy, School of Continuing Education, The University, Canterbury CT2 7NX. Some summer schools are very popular so book early!

Special interest holidays

Contact the English Tourist Board, Thames Tower, Blacks Road, London W6 9EL and Saga Holidays, FREEPOST, Folkestone, Kent CT20 1AZ.

Adult residential colleges

The seven adult residential colleges in England and Wales are for those who missed out on educational opportunities in earlier life, and now want to return to study and live in the college. None of these colleges requires formal entry qualifications; usually an interview, an essay and two or three referees suffice. Minimum entry is around 21 years, but few colleges state an upper age limit. Presently, many students are 30 and 40 year olds, but some are older and it may be just what you are looking for – a chance to find a new direction, gaining a recognised qualification and to experience student life on a full-time basis. Short and part-time non-residential courses are available in many. Courses are frequently in humanities and social sciences, and often lead to higher education and selected professional training. You may be able to obtain financial support covering tuition and living costs once you have a confirmed place at an adult residential college, but as all the educational scene is in the midst of change, check first.

Details can be obtained from:

- Coleg Harlech, Harlech, Gwynedd LL46 2PU
- International Co-Operative College, Stanford Hall, Loughborough, Leics LE12 5QR
- Fircroft College, 1018 Bristol Road, Selly Oak, Birmingham B29 6LH
- Hillcroft College (women only), South Bank, Surbiton, Surrey KT6 6DF
- Northern College, Wentworth Castle, Stainsborough, Barnsley, Yorks S75 3ET
- Plater College (Catholic college), Pullens Lane, Oxford OX3 0DT
- Ruskin College, Walton Street, Oxford OX1 2HE

Traditional university courses

Note that the distinction between polytechnics and universities has now been abolished.

The University of Buckingham

This university is independent, outside the State system, offering first and second degrees. Study is intensive and fees high.

Foreign universities

You can study in EC countries on the same basis as a resident national. Contact the Department of Education and Science for up-to-date information (address below). American and Canadian universities require tests as part of the application process. Contact the Educational Advisory Service, Fulbright Commission, 6 Porter Street, London W1M 2HR for details and information. The Association of Commonwealth Universities can be contacted for information at John Foster House,

36 Gordon Square, London WC1. For details about educational visits and exchanges contact Central Bureau, Seymour Mews House, Seymour Mews, London W1H 9PE.

Note: You may have seen advertisements for American university degrees earned by correspondence course. Whilst many of these are completely respectable and valid, others seem vague. I checked up on one, which turned out to be just an office block without a campus in a City suburb. I would feel less than confident to invest my money in this type of course.

Other possibilities

Try your local museum or art gallery for courses; also nearby leisure centres, health clubs, neighbourhood associations. Some stately homes offer occasional courses, as does the Royal Horticultural Society. Agricultural colleges and similar establishments are worth investigating also. Perhaps your church or synagogue has an adult education programme, or you could attend workshops, seminars, part-time classes through membership of a military association, guild, old school or union. Have you tried your men's or women's club or association? For example, the National Federation of Women's Institutes runs courses for members and their husbands and friends at their adult residential centre Denman College, Marcham, Abingdon, Oxfordshire OX13 6NW. For local information, consult your public reference library.

WHAT CAN YOU STUDY?

Here is a brief glossary.

GCSE The General Certificate of Secondary Education in England and Wales.

A levels and AS levels A levels are usually taken two years after GCSEs. AS levels bridge the gap between the two examinations.

Scottish Certificate of Education   Two levels.

National Vocational Qualifications (NVQs/SVQs in Scotland) are standards of competence agreed by industry in job-specific and general skill areas. They are awarded in a range of broad occupational areas and skill levels. Ordinary and advanced diplomas are to be introduced in 1994.

BTEC (Business and Technology Education Council) awards qualifications at three levels in a wide range of fields plus continuing education courses. SCOTVEC (Scottish Vocational Education Council) offers National and Higher National Certificates.

Royal Society of Arts (RSA) and City and Guilds are two well-recognised awarding bodies for qualifications linked to industry and commerce.

TECs and LECs (Training and Enterprise Councils and Local Enterprise Councils) are independent companies operating in agreement with the Secretary of State for Employment. Includes youth and employment training (YT, ET) and business and enterprise services (see Self-employment Chapter 5).

The Diploma of Higher Education (Cert. HE/Dip. HE) (England and Wales only)   Less well known to both students and employers, the Diploma of Higher Education is an ideal academic 'stepping stone' for adults who prefer to take their time acquiring a flexible qualification. Courses take two years on a full-time basis, three years part-time. Mature students' entry requirements are similar to degree programmes. The Dip HE is comparable in standing to the first two years of an honours degree. This route offers lots of choice: you can go on to further study, if you wish, leading to a suitable degree (employers like this better!) with credit for two years of study or into professional training.

CATS (Credit Accumulation and Transfer)   If you are a mature student with any kind of technical, commercial, para-medical or professional qualification, ask if you might gain credits towards a degree because of it. Consult the Council for National Academic Awards for further information: CNAA, 344–54 Gray's Inn Road, London WC1X 8BP.

APEL (Accredited Prior Experiential Learning) Some universities and colleges have agreed to consider applications from people whose working lives have given them valuable knowledge or experience that directly relates to the content of a degree or higher diploma course. APEL may also give you partial exemption from sections of a degree course.

First degrees At one time, only school or college leavers with particular A levels could be considered for degree programmes. Now mature, unqualified entrants for courses are accepted virtually everywhere, provided they appear likely to be able to cope. Opportunities for mature students are better than ever and you do not always need any academic entry qualifications. Instead, you may be asked to provide evidence of your study ability, but this is very variable and depends on the institution in question. It may be a piece of written work, an Open University course, previous work record, a preparatory course or sampler courses.

Higher degrees include Masters (of Arts, Science, Business Administration (MBA)) and Doctorates. Masters may be taught or earned by research. Part-time and full-time courses are available also by distance learning. Available from universities, business schools, Open University and some correspondence establishments. Doctorates (PhD.) require a minimum of three years' full-time research.

WHAT TO FIND OUT BEFORE ENROLLING IN A COURSE

Before enrolling, take time to consider these factors.

Accreditation

Is the school accredited to a reputable institution? This is particularly important if you are studying towards a certificate, diploma or other paper qualification, or taking on a home study programme. To check qualifications, consult *British Qualifications* (Kogan Page), available in all reference libraries. To find out about a correspondence college, contact the Council for the Accreditation of Correspondence Colleges (CACC), 27 Marylebone Road, London NW1 5JS. The CACC has a free leaflet showing courses and lists of accredited colleges.

Choice

How flexible is the course structure? Could you, for example, change subjects if they do not turn out as expected? Could you sit in on the lectures without taking examinations (this is a useful possibility where training may be restricted to students under 50 years).

Cost (also see Finance, below)

Are grants, concessions, reduced or waived fees available?

Course materials

Will you need to buy special kits, books or other equipment?

Course viability

Enquire if the course continues regardless of student numbers.

Exams

Is the course assessed continually? If so, to what extent do these assessments count towards your final mark? Or, is it examined by project, dissertation, thesis and/or formal examinations?

Facilities

Has the educational establishment adequate library and similar facilities?

Length of course

Check exactly what you are signing up for: a one-day workshop, a ten-week term, a year?

Location

How will you travel to the place of study? Is public transport or car parking available? How long will the journey take?

Prospectus

Always obtain a prospectus from the college and read it carefully.

Time

What is the time commitment of the course? How much homework is there? Is a 'one-day-a-week' course eight, ten or more hours? How many weeks will the course last?

Visits

Whenever possible, make an appointment to visit an institution and talk to one of the staff. Ask about mature student entry requirements, see what life is like as a student. Are there many mature students? What study skill/brush-up help is available? Is the course examined, continually assessed, is there project work? What about career help – is it young person oriented or is there a mature student adviser?

Weather

Will you still feel enthusiastic about the class when it is freezing, foggy, raining, hot or humid?

162

GETTING STARTED AFTER A LONG BREAK

Adult learners have a choice of routes back into education. GCSEs and A levels are the traditional pathways, but there are many more besides. Remember CATS and APEL (see above) which may be just right for you. General preparatory courses abound, all with a variety of methods, contents and quality. Some are intended mainly to build up confidence: others are designed to update skills and may include work experience. Their names are confusing: Returning to Learning, Fresh Start, Access (to Higher Education, Jobs etc.) Taster, Pathway and so on. Most include study skills such as note taking, essay writing and active reading. They tend towards support, counselling and advice rather than formal teaching and are pupil-oriented, i.e. responsive to student needs.

Alternatively, try a short course, either in the subject of your choice or as study preparation. Look in *Time to Learn*, available from National Institute of Adult Continuing Education (NIACE, 19b de Montfort Street, Leicester LE1 7GE). TV Open University programmes can also be helpful.

In addition, obtain study skill help, either on a workshop basis or by distance learning and books. Open University Preparation and Return to Learning courses are available from the National Extension College.

Note: Courses may state that they include something along the lines of career counselling, advice or assessment. While well-qualified vocational personnel exist in many establishments, tutors in other institutions may have only the very briefest of training in careers work. Check the guidelines given in Chapter 1.

APPLYING TO UNIVERSITY

As there is now no distinction between universities and poly-technics, applications for entry to full-time first degrees (not art and design courses) must be made through UCAS (Universities and Colleges Admissions Service).

To apply, you should obtain an entry UCAS application form and handbook from UCAS, PO Box 67, Cheltenham GL50 3SF.

Arts and design courses have separate application procedures. Obtain an Arts and Design Admissions Registry application pack from ADAR, Penn House, 9 Broad Street, Hereford HR4 9AP.

Admission procedures to universities begin in the year prior to entry. Thus, if you wish to apply for a place at university for, say, Autumn 1995, you must obtain application packs from UCAS or ADAR during 1994. They are usually available from early June. The closing date for entries is 15 December.

Other courses usually require direct application to the college in question. Write to the admissions registry for information, stating the course you are interested in.

The situation for post-graduate courses is in the process of change and you may need to check on which system to use. For teaching, try UCAS first; for physiotherapy and art and design, contact directly the establishment whose course you have chosen. Social work has a specialist clearing house: Central Council for Education and Training in Social Work, Derbyshire House, St Chad Street, London WC1H 8AD. Again, check with colleges for updated information. If in doubt, apply directly to individual institutions.

Useful information is available from UCAS, in particular the booklet *University Entrance: mature students*.

GETTING THE BEST OUT OF A COURSE OF STUDY

While you are studying, do not just learn the subject but take every chance to increase your broader knowledge and contacts. Future employment opportunities may well depend as much on the people who know you as the qualifications you gained. This mature student discovered it all too late: 'I spent all my time studying to make sure I'd pass the exams. I didn't socialise or go to meetings or anything that wasn't linked to coursework. Afterwards, when I began looking for a job, I realised I was back to square one – no one around to chat to, no one to ask advice from. How I wish I'd been a bit more friendly and visible . . . no one seems to know I ever existed there.'

Make a point of getting to know the staff as well as fellow students. Even if the tutors are years younger than you, they have experience and contacts in their field. My first psychology job after graduation came about because of one of my past tutors. Acquaint yourself with all the college facilities early on. There are libraries, student services and career professionals. Explore community links, industry and commerce collaborations.

SURVIVING AS A MATURE STUDENT

If you enrol for a correspondence course, the self-discipline you have acquired over the years will stand you in good stead. If you are unsure how you will cope with distance learning, try a sample lesson first – most colleges will be happy to supply this. For traditional, taught courses, try a weekend or 'taster' course to see how you get on before enrolling full-time. It may be possible for you to sit in on a lecture or two, or attend several classes without homework.

For college courses, obtain and read a copy of the students' 'alternative' prospectus. It gives a wry view of student life, plus a wealth of information about clubs and societies: ethnic, religious, political, pressure, community action, music, drama, films, sports. Join the Mature Students' Union to meet others of your age and stage. I found great help and support from the other older students; we shared problems and kept each other going through to finals, and have remained in touch ever since.

Will you fit in with younger people? Yes, you probably will! It is rare to find anyone who does not admire what you are aiming to achieve and age disappears when you are all struggling to get essays in on time. When younger students become homesick or lonely, they often turn to older undergraduates: certainly, I found my junior classmates easier to cope with than my own teenagers!

Family support is invaluable. Partners are usually very proud of their student spouse, but a few find the change hard to take. I have heard many a student (or newly working) wife complain about the necessity to deal with 'His stomach', that is, dinner on the table every night just as before. A few short courses, taken before plunging into a full-time commitment, will not only help you, but prepare partners and families for the change. Teach them to cook (and wash up) at the same time!

One of the big differences from school to university level study, is discovering that you are responsible for your own progress. You learn – the hard way, sometimes! – how to work on your own, meet deadlines, find things out for yourself. Do not despair if you flounder – everybody gets in a muddle at first and soon settles down.

You need a place to study: somewhere to sit and write, and store books and papers which will not be disturbed. Students do a lot of reading. Many of us learned only one way to read and that was to attend to every word. This is not necessarily the best studying method. Learn to skim and scan, then return to those parts which require intensive attention.

Avoid marathon study sessions. Psychologists suggest that attention levels fall after as little as 20 minutes – at most, a couple of hours. Always take a short break to refresh yourself, but leave the ironing, gardening and other time wasters alone!

MONEY

Many day and evening courses have been cut back by local authorities and are much more expensive now than in the past. But this should not deter you. In certain circumstances, you may be able to obtain concessions, reduced or waived fees. Most local authorities make some fee concessions for people over statutory retirement age – usually for non-vocational courses. For full-time study, experts advise students of all ages to make a three-year financial plan, to ensure you do not have to give up half-way through because of money difficulties.

Check the unemployment benefit situation before enrolling on a full-time, three-year course and if you wish to combine part-time study with part-time work. The 21-hour rule applies in some areas. This enables people who are out of work to study up to 21 hours a week without paying fees, provided they remain available for work. But regulations are constantly changing so you must consult your local college or Job Centre for up-to-the-minute information.

From where can you obtain finance? The Department of Education and Science has a helpful booklet: 'Grants to Students, a brief guide'. There are mandatory grants available to anyone who gains a place on a designated course, although certain conditions must be satisfied. A first degree (but not the Open University) usually qualifies for a mandatory grant regardless of age, providing you have not had a grant before. Discretionary grants are available for some further and part-time courses, depending on where you live. Grants are not generally available for post-graduate study. Apply to your local education authority for information on all grants.

Other sources of funding include:

- business enterprise for some TEC courses
- bank loans
- career development loans

If you have training in mind but no money to pay for it, the

Department of Employment, together with several of the commercial banks, may be prepared to finance you. You can borrow between £200 and £5000 to cover part of the fees, books, materials and some living expenses for almost any type of job-related training course lasting up to one year. The loan is interest-free up to three months after your course finishes and repayable over an agreed period. Details are available on 0800 585 505.

Educational charities, bursaries, fellowships and scholarships

Laura Ashley Foundation Awards cover course fees for designated courses to help individual women aged between 18 and 55 who do not have GCSE/O or A levels. Details are available from Laura Ashley Foundation, 33 King Street, London WC2E 8JD.

About 100 travelling fellowships are offered annually by the Winston Churchill Memorial Trust, available to men and women of any age from all walks of life for a non-academic study project abroad. Details from: The Winston Churchill Memorial Trust, 15 Queen's Gate Terrace, London SW7 5PR.

For others, consult *Directory of Grant-making Trusts* (in libraries); also *Second Chances* (COIC).

USEFUL HELP AND INFORMATION

The Department of Education and Science, Elizabeth House, York Road, London SE1 7PH.

Degree Course Guides about individual course details, entry requirements, career exits etc. Published by CRAC Publications, Hobsons Ltd, Batemen Street, Cambridge CB2 1LZ.

ECCTIS (0242 518724) is a *free* national computerised information service with information on thousands of courses leading to recognised qualifications and credit transfers.

Educational Guidance units for Adults (EGA) provides *free* information on education and training for adults nationwide. The *Directory of Educational Guidance Services for Adults* can be obtained from ECCTIS at the above address; local details also in *Second Chances*.

PICKUP is intended to help people at work update their skills.

TAP is a data base of training and educational opportunities. Find out more via Job Centres.

Some areas have local authority **Educational Shops**, which offer excellent information for adult learners.

7

The Over 50s' Self-Marketing Tool Kit

BY NOW, YOU SHOULD HAVE A GOOD IDEA of your own resources and the options available in paid positions, self-employment, gift work and second chance study. Next, you will want to get in touch with an organisation, employer, trader or institution. Whatever you seek – a job, business, goods, contracts, a place on a course – will require effective self-marketing material.

Good preparation helps over 50s to make the most of their most valuable assets: experiences, skills and abilities. If you have followed my earlier recommendations, you will be familiar with your special talents and ready to start on application forms, a CV, covering letters, a job search and an interview strategy.

But, if you have skipped through the pages and are in such a hurry to get into a job that you want to start here – *stop now!* You may be wasting a precious opportunity, so return to Chapter 2 and complete the self-assessment exercises now.

It is important to understand that, while untrained youngsters may fill in their CV in a matter of minutes, mature folk need to take their time. Your 30+ working years cannot be described in just a sentence or two. Unlike raw recruits who must expand their achievements, your life story would fill a book and must be condensed. You need to select and highlight your best experiences, and your most relevant attributes, then transform them into a polished, attention-holding vehicle which says, loud and clear: 'Here is someone special, we must interview him/her'.

The self-marketing tool kit includes:

- how to create your own CV
- which CV format is right for you
- what employers look for in a CV
- what to do about age on your CV
- CV presentation, style and language
- application forms
- accompanying letters
- finding job vacancies
- ten point plan for networking and contacts
- types of interview
- strategies for interviews
- handling age questions at interviews
- selection tests
- dealing with salary
- help and advice

HOW TO CREATE YOUR OWN CURRICULUM VITAE

They keep asking me to send a CV. I don't think I've ever had to write one; if I did, it was 30 years ago and I've forgotten all about it. I went straight from school into Articles and stayed with the same firm all my working life.

Accountant, voluntary retired, mid 50s

An effective CV is the most important piece of paper you will ever create – and, possibly, the most worrying. A clear, well-presented CV can open doors, jog memories, revitalise careers, create an image and gain interviews.

Recruiters receive hundreds of CVs for just *one* job vacancy. At best, your application may receive just a fleeting glance from the office junior for a few seconds. You are in competition with youngsters, present employees and everyone else who is keen to get back to work.

Your CV tells the recruiter a lot about you: if it is poorly presented, old fashioned, out of date, grubby or long-winded, they will assume you are the same – and it will go straight into the wastepaper basket. But, if it is crisp, clean, concise, well organised, relevant to the job vacancy, bright and positive, you stand a better chance of getting to interview and, hopefully, to the job itself.

Who needs a CV? Everyone – yes, all of you! Whatever your future plans, regardless of pay, position or prospects, you need a CV. In the past, you may have thought a CV was only for highly qualified professionals or senior managers. Today, it is an essential calling card for each and every individual. It saves lengthy explanations, promotes job applications, informs network contacts, proves one's case, documents evidence and provides a credible image.

Let us look, for a moment, at what a CV is and is not. A CV is a selected overview, in summary form, of your occupational history. It is most commonly – but not exclusively – concerned with employment. The purpose of a CV is *to obtain an interview*. It is not meant to land you a job, but is only one means to that end.

Take note of what a CV is not: *not* your unabridged life story; *not* a family tree detailing all your ancestors and grandchildren; *not* a record of every piece of paper you've ever gained; *not* a platform for your views on the world; *not* an English language essay.

Despite what you may have read in those small ads offering 'instant' or 'professional' CVs, there are no guarantees in the CV business. There is no such thing as the 'right' or 'perfect' CV. Your style is special, your circumstances unique. Some employers say they can spot a ready-made CV immediately and throw it straight into the wastepaper basket; others argue it is the CV contents which matter most, not the expensive laser printer. Before you decide to spend money on a prepared CV, do try to create your own. If you already have a prepared CV to hand, personalise it with some word of your own – a good thesaurus is really all you need!

As a career counsellor, I am often asked to help clients with their CV. My advice is usually this: I will prepare a framework for you, and illustrate the various formats and language. But, it is your personal CV, one which – hopefully – will form the basis for an interview. Include information which *you* are prepared to discuss, *you* feel confident enough to elaborate on and which *you* can explain to the interviewer. Following the guidelines below, tailor your CV to suit your circumstances.

There are three parts to this section on CVs: the first looks at the various types of CV; next, there are tips and guidelines for your CV contents – what to include, what may be omitted; finally, there is a short section on CV presentation, style and language.

Always remember, the purpose of a CV is to get you an interview, not a job.

CV FORMATS

Choose from the following formats.

- **Chronological** This is the CV format you were probably taught at school or college, providing a skeleton outline of your educational and employment history, starting with education and qualifications, continuing with previous work history in date order and ending with referees. Additional information lists skills, interests or hobbies and occasionally there is a mention of salary. The most common length is one or two A4 pages. It is popular with employers mainly because they are accustomed to it. The main disadvantage to you, the job-seeker, is that time gaps are easily spotted and your age is all too apparent.

- **Functional** While functional CVs have drawbacks, they pay no attention to any career breaks and quickly capture the reader's interest. This format highlights skills and achievements in a few brief statements under theme headings. For example, Financial Management, General Accounting, Communication Skills, Commercial Sense. Headings are related to the type of work you want to do – for a managerial application, you might show supervision, administrative, organisational and planning skills. The information is always accurate, factual and concise, and usually includes details of employers, job description and duration of work. *But*, functional CVs are harder to write and read, and sometimes make employers wary.

- **Mixed/combination format** Here an employment history is grouped under two or three general headings. A brief, chronological work history may follow, perhaps without dates.

Which CV format is right for you?

If you have a solid work history, good credentials, no employment gaps and a good fit between the job description and your own educational achievements – use a *chronological format*.

If you have an erratic work history, lots of time gaps, many different or temporary jobs, or if you want to switch to a new career or level – use a *functional format*.

If you have just a few interruptions in your work history (no more than two or three) and you want to include non-paid work as regular employment – use the *mixed format*.

What you must include in your CV

- **Contact details** Your full name, address (remember the post code), home telephone code and number (state if you have an answerphone). Type your name in CAPITAL LETTERS, use **bold type** sparingly if you have it.

- **A career summary** Samuel N. Ray, an American outplacement expert, suggests that you 'hook' an employer's attention with a crisp, clear, short summary of your positive

174

attributes at the top of a résumé. Now, there is a big difference between the British CV and American résumé, and you may decide this is not appropriate for you. But, I feel it is a very worthwhile approach to concise writing and active presentation of your particular strengths and experience. Go back to the 'Self-Portrait' section of Chapter 2 (pages 54–5) to discover if you can make use of it as a career summary.

- **Employment history** Start with your most recent employment and describe your work experience *backwards*: i.e. starting with the most recent employment. Indicate how long you were in each job; give the company's name and describe briefly what it does.

- For each employment, give a **descriptive job title** first. Do not just say 'Marketing Manager'. Instead, what or whom did you manage – Sales? Advertising? Be specific.

- **State your responsibilities** for each job. Go back to your own job description, or visit the library for books such as *The Penguin Careers Guide* or *Occupations 93*, where you will find useful job descriptions. Use action verbs (see CV Presentation, below) avoiding the phrase 'responsibilities included' which becomes very tedious after six repetitions.

- **State your achievements** in the job. What did you do that made a difference? If your answer is 'Nothing', go back to the self-assessment exercises and rework your skills inventory. Achievements could include how profits increased, sales increased, training programmes were brought in and problems solved.

- Specify your job titles only for jobs you held a long time ago. Do not elaborate about jobs you had more than 15 or 20 years ago.

- Avoid any explanations about why you are presently unemployed, unless it is very recent and absolutely not your fault, e.g. 'Available due to business closure'.

- Include **education and training details only if recent and relevant** to the job. Do not give particulars of school certificate results, O and A level grades, degree course contents. If necessary, give higher education details only (no dates unless within past ten years) in one line. For example, BSc (Economics), 2.i., University of London.

Other things you may want to include

- Evidence of computer skills, financial abilities, (up-to-date) technical know-how, company training, apprenticeship (recent).

- Professional memberships and associations – if relevant.

- Publications – again, only if relevant to the job. If the list is long, attach details on a separate sheet.

- Community activities – only if the prospective employer indicates an interest in the job advertisement (also see below).

- Driving licence, foreign languages (state proficiency level), computer literacy (state programmes), first aid – if relevant.

- Employment objective (type of work you are looking for).

- Awards, recognitions, promotions.

- Your date of birth and your present age: *see below.*

What to omit

- Nicknames.

- All pronouns (I, we, they, you) and articles (a, an, the).

- Details about size and age of dependants.

- Details about spouse or partner.

- Past employer's address, telephone number.

- Anything to do with marital status.

- Anything to do with race.

- Anything to do with religion.

- Physical details (height, weight, state of health).

- Salary requirements.

- Referees' names and contact details – 'References available' is usually enough.

- Hobbies/interest not relevant to the job.

- Think twice about adding short courses on human relation-type topics (counselling, interpersonal skills and so on), unless they are directly linked to the job.

Leave out anything whatsoever to do with:

- astrological signs, lucky numbers, favourite colours, diet and fitness details

- beloved books, pet, flowers, dance tunes

- residential details (mortgage – or lack of, second home, cardboard city)

- marital difficulties ('in process of divorce')

- anything sexist

- out-of-date phrases

WHAT EMPLOYERS LOOK FOR IN A CV

When you think about applications from an employer's point of view, you soon realise that it makes sense to provide a clean, error-free, legible CV. Imagine ploughing through the hundreds of pieces of paper, some 50+ pages long, others merely 10 poorly scrawled lines; there are the garish or flashy pieces, ones with cartoons, weird qualifications or in foreign languages, the badly written or misspelt, those with the umpteen photographs, copies of O-level certificates or cycling proficiency tests! Take heed, then, of the suggestions below on presentation, style and language.

Vacancies exist because an employer has a problem to overcome and wishes to solve it in the most efficient way possible. Your task, as an applicant, is to illustrate how swiftly and smoothly you can answer the problem by matching your skills and experience to the employer's needs. And you will illustrate it best of all with a clean, clear CV.

An employer's time, temper and tastebuds (and your chances of success) are improved by sending along a CV which:

- omits anything off-putting (e.g. age, date of birth);

- includes all these basic ingredients;
  - who you are and where you can be contacted,
  - what you have been doing,
  - proof that you can do it,
  - what knowledge you possess,
  - proof that you have it;

- says all of the above while stressing the benefits of interviewing you.

FURTHER POINTS ABOUT CVs

What to do about age

In my book for relocating partners, *Portable Careers*, I included a short section about age in self-marketing material which is reproduced below, together with some additional points.

Keep in mind, however, two major points.

1. The aim of a CV or résumé is to gain an interview.
2. Your CV objective is to solve an employer's problem. By offering personal information at too early a stage, you may only add to the employer's problem (and yours).

Over 40s, women, minority groups, trailing spouses, disabled people, all find paid employment difficult because of myths and prejudice. In some countries (USA, France, Canada) it is illegal to ask questions about age (or race, religion or ethnic group) on application material or interviews. Sadly, the UK has not adopted these sensible measures yet. In the mean time, here are some tips and suggestions for overcoming questions about age/date of birth in CVs or application forms. Do remember, though, the choice is yours – the results are not guaranteed!

- Attach a (flattering) photograph.

- Write 'Not Applicable', 'Over 21' or similar instead of age details.

- Omit age information altogether.

- Write 'See accompanying letter' and include your details there.

- Never describe yourself as 'retired' or 'out of work'.

- Don't apologise – don't write 'I'm a young 55!'

- Place your most recent or relevant experience immediately after your name; follow with your remaining work history in reverse order, then educational details. Place personal contact information at the end – without a date of birth or similar.

- All educational information should exclude dates.

- Emphasise your assets: your ability to work with others, maturity, good customer contacts, loyalty, reliability, sense of responsibility. Say how well you delegate, cope with change, manage others, make good decisions, keep cool. Give evidence of what you are good at, not just a long list of adjectives!

- Others say that older people should not hide their age, but should make far more effort to sell themselves.

- Concentrate the reader's attention on your strengths: good literacy skills, balanced loyalties, open-mindedness, tolerance, cross-cultural experience, adaptability, self-discipline, good education. Don't just say you are 'flexible'; illustrate the point with a work-related example.

- Do not undervalue yourself. If an applicant applies for a job in a lower than expected salary range, some recruiters believe they are either desperate or useless.

- Indicate a motivated, positive attitude to the job. Show an interest in current affairs, business matters, education, environment, economics, computers.

- Imply good physical and mental health and fitness: mention bridge, crosswords, chess; active team participation, golf and similar sports, committee work, voluntary posts of responsibility, research projects, Rotary and similar memberships.

- Mention advanced driving licence, computer familiarity, proficient languages and special skills. Include course details if you are presently studying and indicate expected achievements – example: 'Degree expected, Summer, 1994.'

- Always aim to be informed and informative, up to date and positive.

CV presentation

Tailor your CV to the requirements of the job. Present yourself well: use good-quality paper, plenty of space between items, good margins, clear headings. Type (with a new ribbon) or word process on unlined pale (preferably white) paper. A ring binder, spiral band or coloured cover may draw attention and look attractive, but it is the contents which count. A length of one page is ideal; two or three well-spaced sheets are acceptable; any more is *too long*.

It is unnecessary to construct beautiful, grammatically elegant sentences. The aim is to present effective information to hold the employer's attention. Omit pronouns such as I, we, they, you; also leave out articles (the, a, an) to make your writing crisp. Instead, use short, punchy, positive *action words*

for immediate impact. Action words are active verbs such as the
following.

ACTION VERBS

Administered	Advanced	Ameliorated	Analysed
Anticipated	Approved	Assembled	Augmented
Budgeted			
Calculated	Catalogued	Changed	Chose
Combated	Combined	Commanded	Conducted
Constructed	Consulted	Contracted	Controlled
Convinced	Co-operated	Co-ordinated	Counselled
Created	Commercialised	Communicated	Concluded
Decentralised	Decided	Defined	Delegated
Delineated	Designed	Determined	Developed
Directed	Discovered	Distributed	Diversified
Educated	Elaborated	Enlarged	Entertained
Envisaged	Equalised	Established	Evaluated
Examined	Expand	Experimented	Exploited
Explored	Exported	Extrapolated	
Facilitated	Farmed	Fashioned	Figured
Furthered	Finalised	Financed	Fixed
Followed	Founded	Functioned	Fused
Gained	Gathered	Governed	Guided
Halted	Halved	Handled	
Harmonised	Headed	Heightened	
Identified	Improved	Interpreted	Interviewed
Implemented	Imported	Imposed	Invented
Incited	Incorporated	Incremented	Informed
Innovated	Improvised	Invested	Installed
Instructed	Integrated	Interested	
Joined	Justified		
Lead	Levelled	Linked	
Made	Maintained	Managed	Marketed
Mounted	Manoeuvred	Modernised	Motivated

Negotiated	Normalised		
Observed	Obtained	Organised	Oriented
Participated	Persuaded	Piloted	Planned
Prepared	Presented	Presided	Produced
Progammed	Projected	Promoted	Proposed
Put in place			
Raised	Rationalised	Read	Realised
Recommended	Reconstructed	Recruited	Rectified
Redressed	Reformed	Regulated	Reinforced
Rejected	Repaired	Represented	Revised
Researched	Reunited		
Sanctioned	Scrutinised	Selected	Signed
Sold	Solicited	Stocked	Studied
Structured	Subscribed	Suggested	Supervised
Surveyed	Synthesised	Systematised	
Tested	Transformed	Translated	Transported
Used			
Visited			
Was promoted	Won	Worked	Wrote

Use the language an employer will recognise. Translate specialised activities into words linked to the employment vacancy. If you are an ex-military person, for example, Battalion PRO will mean nothing to recruiters in public relations. Similarly, systems analysis jargon may be meaningless to a social work organisation. Domestic, homemaking terminology is undervalued by commercial concerns. Describe what you have done in simple, lucid terms which make sense to the recruiter.

Those re-entering the workplace after a gap express concern about describing and including non-paid experience in a CV. My advice is simple: include all unpaid, *quality* work, such as committee participation, school governing, public presentations, sport sponsorship etc., whenever you can. Emphasise your contribution, demonstrate what you achieved that made a

182

difference. But, if you poured tea or licked envelopes for how-ever worthy a cause – omit it until the interview and then include if and when the time is right.

At the risk of overstatement, here it is again. Include achieve-ments *that are related to the job*.

Finally, check and check again for spelling errors, the right enclosures, your signature and correct postage stamps.

APPLICATION FORMS

The first thing to do with a predesigned application form is to photocopy it. Do not put a mark on it until you have at least one, preferably two, spare copies. Then, sit down and read through all the questions and instructions, if any, extremely carefully. If it has been thoughtfully constructed, the front page will contain your personal data: name, contact details etc. The following pages (usually education, training and employment history) will be photocopied and distributed for use at interview.

What are you asked to do? Complete every section or selected ones? Write or type? Use ink or biro? Black or blue? Look at all the small print and follow the instructions to the proverbial letter.

On one of your copies, begin filling in the easiest parts – your name, address etc. Then, consider the Educational and Pre-vious Employment sections. Many application forms ask for full details of every single school and job. In certain cirumstances, this may be completely appropriate, but in other situations, consider grouping together anything more than 15 years old. For instance, if I were to apply now for a sales job with a craft company (one of my passions is needlecraft), I should not go into detail about my 1950s School Certificate. Instead, I should write this – Education: all public examinations up to and includ-ing Bachelor degree.

What should you write in the section(s) asking for 'Any Other Relevant Information' and/or 'Reasons why you should be considered for the post'? This is your opportunity to blow your own trumpet a little. Read the job description or advertisement once. Then, explain accurately how your special advantages match the skills and abilities required. You may have to do this several times to get it right but do not worry, take your time. I have a special regard for employers, such as the Automobile Association, who invite applicants 'to include previous unpaid experience, e.g. domestic duties, voluntary activities and any leisure interests'.

When you feel satisfied with your draft attempts, complete the original application form, remembering any special instructions. Check the spelling and enclosures. Photocopy it and file away for use at the interview. Even if you have completed an application form for a job, it is a good idea to include a copy of your CV. And do not forget to place the correct amount of postage on the envelope!

ACCOMPANYING AND THANK-YOU LETTERS

Letters are used to accompany application forms and CVs when pursuing a contact or referral, making a 'cold' call, applying for a job or following an interview. These letters are short and to the point, with only three or four paragraphs. They are written in concise, business language, avoiding a casual or over-friendly tone. Address an individual whenever possible. To find a named person, consult company reports, publicity or advertisements, or ask the telephonist. Keep a copy of your letter for future reference. There are three main ingredients.

- **Opening paragraphs** State why you are writing. Are you asking for information, looking for an informal interview, writing at someone else's suggestion? Then state this at the start. Leave out wordy opening pleasantries. Mention a mutual contact and any recent and relevant publicity about the firm if you want, but get down to the nitty-gritty as soon as possible.

- **Central portion** Highlight your special skills and experience. There is no need to repeat your entire CV here, merely reiterate what is unique about you. Use positive language to illustrate simply why you would be a valuable employee or worth spending time interviewing. This section is also the place to clarify any CV or application form matters (about age, stage, qualifications or anything else).

- **Final paragraph** Say what you want to happen next: you look forward to an interview, value the opportunity to meet, will telephone for an appointment, appreciate the time given.

Unsolicited job search letters ask for either genuine general information about a company or indirectly invite suggestions about job prospects. Never ask for work directly. The goal is to obtain a short interview or informal chat with an employee in the know who may be able to signpost you towards a vacancy. Assist the reader with a short, but concrete, overview of your skills and experience. Vague, general letters are unlikely to achieve a job. 'Yes, I do have jobs,' a personnel executive explained to me, 'But I cannot begin to match a person with a vacancy if I don't know what they can do. They must tell me something about themselves first.'

FINDING JOB VACANCIES

First, here is a warning. Never pay money to anyone advertising job opportunities or offering help in seeking a job, unless you are sure they are acting legally. The Employment Agencies Act 1973 makes it illegal for anyone in the business of finding or seeking to find people jobs (except in rare cases such as the entertainment and modelling industries) to charge those people for doing so. Almost all employment agencies must be licensed by the Department of Employment. If you have any doubts about an advertisement or agency, contact your nearest Job Centre.

The key to a successful job search is *visibility*. People out there in the world of work must know about you and it is up to you to remind them – by your physical presence, telephone, letters and any other correspondence – of your existence, expertise and experience. But, if your wonderful CV and beautifully crafted letter sits gathering dust while you become a recluse, you become *invisible*. If political memory lasts a mere six weeks, my guess is that unemployment memory is considerably less. It only takes a few days for an office, workshop or trading floor to forget past employees, so your first task is to maintain visibility.

However, take great care not to make a nuisance of yourself! Pestering, begging, harassing, badgering, pleading or anything similar is counter-productive. Absence, in the world of work, rarely makes the heart grow fonder, but too much of a good person may kill it off absolutely.

Jobs may be located through the following means.

Advertisements

Job vacancies are advertised in the national and local press, magazines, professional and trade journals, as well as all sorts of unexpected places like radio stations, TV Teletext, shop windows and supermarket notice boards. Inspect all advertisements, as positions may be placed in a variety of categories. Use your main reference library if you want to avoid a large newsagents' bill.

Analyse the blurb very carefully indeed. Advertisements tend to be worded with an 'ideal' candidate in mind. Do not worry if you cannot meet every single requirement. Older workers should not be deterred by advertised age limits as the organisation may be seeking the right person for the job rather than a particular age. Always reply if your qualifications and experience meet most of the vacancy needs. If it is a very detailed brief, search out the 'musts' from the 'preferred'. *Musts* are phrases such as: 'Must be fluent in Japanese'; 'Previous accounting experience essential'; 'Substantial man-management experience necessary'. *Preferreds* are such phrases as: 'A keen interest in . . .' 'Some knowledge of . . . useful'; 'Previous experience an advantage'.

Those in the know say you should not rush to respond to an advertisement. As the first avalanche will be sifted through quickly, the next lot may be considered more carefully. Let the dust settle for a couple of days after the advertisement appears and then post your reply.

Contacts

Networking and contacts are an excellent method of job searching, providing you heed the remarks below. Never restrict yourself to finding a job solely through advertisements as this is the lowest, smallest, least likely way of getting a job. Contacts are people who may open doors for you, either directly if they have vacancies or indirectly by referring you to someone else.

You have no contacts? Use the following list for ideas about where contacts may be found:

enthusiasts' clubs
family and relatives
conference participants
job club
local shopkeepers
military organisations
neighbours and community
  persons
old boys/girls associations
past employers
past polytechnic/university
  friends
personal friends
previous suppliers or
  customers
professional acquaintances

professional institutes
recreational clubs
Rotary clubs, Freemasons
self-help group
sports club friends
the hairdresser/barber
trade associates
veterans associations
voluntary institutions
work colleagues
workshop/seminar members
your bank, accountant,
  lawyer
your doctor, dentist,
  optician, vet
your priest, minister, rabbi.

Guidelines for using contacts

A great deal has been written and spoken about the value of networking and contacts for job-hunters. From the 'old boys' network' and once-upon-a-schoolmate, through to umpteen groups and associations for minorities, professionals, people-in-Company X and similar. There now exists, I believe, much confusion over just how and what to do about networking.

Everybody uses contacts during their lives – we all have relations, friends and acquaintances to whom we are linked. We belong to religious, social, sporting, community, educational, hobby, military, trade, health and many other groups. So, unless you are an orphan recluse, living incommunicado on an uninhabited island, there will always be people who know you as well as people you know. Some individuals will be closely acquainted to you; others may be less familiar. But, according to some experts, all are fair game when it comes to getting a job.

I do not believe that it is a good idea to get in touch with everyone you have ever known in your life to ask them for a job. Indeed, few would recommend such an action. But there seems to be a generalised notion around that this is what you do. It is sometimes hard to convey a word of caution without sounding unduly off-putting. Below is a Ten-point Plan for Networking and Contacts, which will help you go about networking in an effective way.

Ten-point plan for networking and contacts

1. Never ask contacts for a *job*, only ask for *information*. Using networking and contacts to plead or beg for work is a fast route to being shown the door and losing all your friends. Constantly busy telephone signals, unreturned answering machine messages, secretarial stonewalling and delayed responses to letters add up to the same thing: rejection. If you abuse the system by asking for a job, many others may suffer unnecessarily.

2. Most people like to help out their friends, family and

colleagues, especially if they are approached diplomatically and tactfully. They need to feel appreciated afterwards.

3. Keep in touch with your contacts – do not just use them when you want something. Instead, maintain them on a (light) social basis, give them an occasional lunch or piece of good news, send a congratulatory note if you hear of a success.

4. In the wise words of the old adage: 'Don't tread on anyone on the way up because you may need them on the way down'.

5. Keep interviews or telephone calls short and well spaced. No one useful has the time to spare to listen to your life story or talk to you at length several times a day. Prepare what you want to say beforehand, say how long you expect to be and stick to it. Keep calm and polite, enquire if it is a convenient time to speak; if not, offer to call back at a more favourable moment. Do not take an unfriendly reply personally: you cannot know what is going on in the other person's office at the time of your call, so do not react negatively or become a nuisance to someone whose co-operation you need.

6. Send a thank-you letter after an interview; sound appreciative but not overly deferential. Send a similar letter to the person who gave you the contact.

7. Ask if you can do anything in return.

8. Do not assume friendship where it does not exist. If you met Bloggs Minor at prep school in 1940-something, or were one of the Class of '51, do not expect to be remembered.

9. Respect the limits of specialist contacts who may be precluded from giving out information because of professional ethics and/or confidentiality.

10. In professional or voluntary associations, offer to do something more than attend a meeting once a year. Being an active member increases your contacts and your visibility.

'Hidden' job market

This is often referred to in advertisements placed by career or outplacement consultancies to suggest they have access to jobs obtained through word of mouth or via contacts. There are differences of opinion on this tricky topic: some say it is just a marketing ploy, intended to lure the unsuspecting and vulnerable into parting with a lot of money in order to obtain vague information. Others say it was a blessing which they would not have been without. The main message seems to be this: check any advertisement making big promises extremely carefully indeed; do not pay for anything you cannot afford; and keep your own job search going all the time.

Agencies and bureaux

You should not have to pay for an introduction to work from an employment agency. Look for a bureau which works for an employer and is a member of a reputable, national association. Ask your friends if they have had contact with the agency and with whom they dealt.

Generally, agencies are good for specialised work or for short-term employment. They cannot work miracles, but often provide good starting points for clarifying your goals and providing opportunities you may not have considered.

Specialised agencies for the over 50s have come and gone, along with many other businesses during the early 1990s.

Headhunters

Ideally, headhunters, executive or management recruiters should be able to open more doors for you than you can ever do yourself. They can offer up-to-the-minute information on the job market, steer you towards good self-marketing techniques, provide introductions and feedback. Less than useful are those headhunters who make lots of encouraging sounds until you say your age and then have an unexpected, urgent appointment elsewhere. Avoid, too, those who gush enthusiastically, but then say you are 'over-qualified'.

You need to be flexible and realistic with a headhunter. Be prepared to negotiate and offer only what you know you can do – not what you believe might be possible. A reliable recruiter will require your up-to-date CV. Take any advice offered and revise it accordingly. References may also be requested.

Others

Employment agencies

Usually for junior and lower management grades. Some are general, others specialise (accountancy staff, secretaries).

Executive registers

Consultancy-type operations which advertise for employers on a regular basis.

Career counsellors

Many advertise themselves as having access to the 'hidden' or 'not advertised' job market. As a rule, they are contacted by companies to keep an eye open for potentially interesting executives. You will have to pay fees for their services and I suggest you take along a large pinch of salt if they claim huge success rates, e.g. 90 per cent placed in three months.

Executive search

See Headhunters, above.

Useful directories

The Grapevine Recruitment Library contains five annual publications, available at most reference libraries. There are directories of:

- *International Recruitment Consultants*
- *Interim Management and Non Executive Directors*
- *Career Management, Outplacement and Assessment*
- *Executive and Management Development Consultants*
- *Executive Recruitment Consultants*

TYPES OF INTERVIEW

You may encounter many different types of interview. Here is a list of the main ones.

- **Directive interviews** Here the interviewers follow a defined pattern for all interviewees. They ask specific to-the-point questions in a predesigned pattern and have a checklist to follow with a response sheet for comparing everyone's answers later.

- **Non-directive** interviews are loosely structured, broad and general, with many 'open-ended' types of question. They may begin with a 'Tell me/us about yourself' question which can be quite off-putting. Instead of blundering about, prepare in advance a short (one or two minutes is enough) overview of your background. This kind of interview may be genuine, but it could also be very deceptive. The pleasant, benign beginning could be a softening-up preamble to something more stressful. Keep your wits about you.

- **Stress interviews** are relatively uncommon, but when they are used, their aim is to discover how the interviewee reacts under pressure. A stress interview can involve silence, challenge, confrontation, unfriendliness, brusqueness, staring. An interviewee may be subjected to considerable rudeness from one interviewer only or from several. The trick here is to stay unruffled and composed. Do not allow yourself to be distressed, angry or intimidated. Do not stare at your shoes, tap your fingers or fidget. Take some deep breaths and try to

192

collect yourself. Look pleasant and expectant and smile. Interrupt, if necessary, by saying 'Wait a minute, let's go one step at a time . . . could you repeat the question, please?'

- **Group interviews** are when several candidates are interviewed together by one or several interviewers. In a business context, it often takes the form of a group discussion or exercise(s) with the interviewers acting as observers to monitor each candidate's contribution. There are few set rules for group interviews.

- **Board interviews** consist of one interviewee and several interviewers. It is most common in high-level corporate positions. Try to establish rapport with one of the board rather than talking to everyone.

- **Screening interviews** are the first rung of the employment ladder, conducted by someone from personnel and intended to find out more general information about you from your CV or application form.

- **Employment interviews** are usually the second round of interviews with the people with whom you will actually be working. Here, your knowledge and experience will be tested. In between each round, you may be asked to take selection tests – more about them later.

Strategies for interviews

When did you last attend an interview? If it is many years ago, you may be feeling nervous, apprehensive and even sick. Here are some simple strategies to raise your confidence.

Your aim at interview is to sell yourself as an enthusiastic, sincere, tactful and courteous potential employee. You must *demonstrate* these qualities by what you say and how you say it – your words, actions, behaviour. Aim to leave a favourable impression; make the interviewer feel good about you.

Interviews of any variety start at home. Check the location of the interview, transportation and travel time. Avoid shopping *en route*; do not bring plastic bags, pets or children. Take an umbrella if necessary, but leave it outside the interview room. Bring a notebook and pen, write down a prompt or two for any important questions you want to ask.

Remember the interviewer's name. Find out all you can about the company or organisation before you attend the interview. For commercial organisations, there are company reports, directories and similar material available from business and public libraries. Some areas have video data company reports, so ask at your local careers office. Help may also be available from job clubs which carry major directories.

Aim to arrive at the venue five or ten minutes early – no more, but never late. Avoid lunchtime interviews: they are outdated opportunities for a booze-up and, besides, older individuals tend to be fresher in the early part of the day. If a catastrophe or a genuine emergency occurs, telephone immediately to explain the delay and ask for another appointment.

Refresh your memory from copies of your application form, CV, covering letters and the job advertisement. Prepare answers to fill in any gaps.

Personal appearance matters. To present a positive, energetic image, get a good night's sleep beforehand, avoid alcohol and smoking, and wear businesslike clothes. Do not forget your spectacles if you need them. Take note of the remarks in Chapter 1 about keeping healthy, smart and in shape.

Be pleasant from the moment you open the door and walk towards the receptionist, who may well be involved in the selection process. When invited into the interview room, stand upright, smile, establish eye contact and shake hands firmly. Leave everything, apart from a briefcase and/or handbag, outside. Sit down only when and where you are invited.

Body language is an important indicator. Sit well back into a chair, not on the edge of the seat. Do not grip the chair tightly, slouch or slump, peer at the interviewer, move closer, pick or fiddle with things. Keep your shoulders down and your arms away from your body and your head up – nobody is going to hit you, besides, covering and hiding yourself are signs of tension.

Think more about the interviewer than yourself. Show you are listening and paying attention by keeping eye contact (not staring, though) with the speaker, and giving encouraging nods now and then. When it is your turn to speak, answer questions without giving a lecture or monologue. If you need time to think of a reply, do so but only in moderation. If the interviewer yawns or looks bored – you have failed!

Above all, never, ever belittle past employers or colleagues. If you are asked why you left your last job, give a simple, unbiased reason. Do not complain, either, about your family, ex-spouse, the government or state of the world today.

Over 50s should be especially careful to use non-sexist language and not outdated phrases. Do not call a woman 'love', 'sweetie' or 'my dear' – she may be the managing director. Eliminate phrases such as 'When I was younger . . .', 'In my day . . .', 'Years ago . . .'. Do not talk about your wartime experiences, how little/much you earned when you were younger or your grandchildren.

Towards the end of the interview, you will be asked if you have any questions: prepare some in advance. Find out about the post's previous employee – why did he/she leave, what were his/her responsibilities, are the current ones similar or different? Remember those useful openers: What? Where? Who? When? Why? and How?

Handling age questions at interviews

Re-entry women with whom I have worked are experienced in dealing with awkward questions at interviews. Despite legislation, they often find themselves facing questions about childcare, husbands, domestic priorities and family matters. They feel trapped; it is a no-win situation. If they refuse to answer, they will probably fail the interview; if they answer honestly, the result is most likely to be the same. Should they decide instead to bend the truth a little, it makes them uncomfortable and if they argue the validity of the question, they are labelled as 'aggressive'.

Similarly, older workers face awkward interview questions about their age. Sometimes there are more subtle comments such as 'We are a young team', 'How old are your children?' or

'You seem over-qualified'. What do you say then? There are several ways to handle face-to-face questions about age.

- **Choice No. 1** Face the question squarely. If you are asked directly for your age or date of birth, give the information in a polite, unruffled voice. Do not comment, qualify or enlarge on the topic. Try to move the interview on to another topic swiftly.

- **Choice No. 2** Object! Refuse to answer! Be aware, though, that at present the UK has no legislation against age discrimination, so it is perfectly legitimate for an employer to ask these questions. You could also ignore the question, but whatever you do, be quite clear in your own mind of the possible risks and consequences of your refusal.

- **Choice No. 3** Challenge the issue: when asked for your age, say, firmly 'I think you are really asking me how long I am going to stay in the job . . .' Staying unflappable, evading the awkward questions and remaining poised will often produce a better impression than getting huffy or submitting under pressure.

SELECTION TESTS

Many of you will have seen, or even tried your hand at, magazine questionnaires which claim to test everything from the state of your love life to your word processing quotient. They are simple to do and it is fun to read the so-called 'results' afterwards. They are not, however, anything like the tests used for selection and recruitment. These psychometric tests – statistically validated written tests – are becoming increasingly common in the recruitment process.

In 1988, a survey found that between a quarter and a third of *The Times* 1000 biggest companies used psychological tests as part of their selection procedure and the number was expected to increase. Now, several years later and in a much tougher economic climate, the chances of you, the applicant, facing a battery of tests at selection are even higher.

From one viewpoint, formalised selection procedures may be said to reduce discrimination and unfairness. Pen and paper tests will not notice if your hair is grey, you need reading glasses or have lots of laughter lines. At informal interviews – the Equal Opportunities Commission does not recommend these – individuals may be judged on subjective, possibly prejudiced criteria, leading to many false assumptions. However, there is potential for misuse of all selection procedures, including those with structured tests.

You may be concerned if you are requested to take tests during a selection. Certainly you may feel particularly apprehensive if you have never completed these procedures before or think of them as a kind of modernised '11-plus' examination. Put such thoughts aside!

Selection tests fall into two broad categories. *Aptitude tests* set out to measure our capacity to acquire skills and knowledge. They are often presented as a 'battery', that is, a group of related tests. One example is the Morrisby Differential Test Aptitude Battery, which provides a guide to solving new problems, and reasoning with word, numbers and visual material. The test also identifies special occupational skills such as mechanical aptitudes and accuracy in checking details. Aptitudes are often tested against a stopwatch. Do not worry if you do not complete them or if you run out of time. Generally speaking, aptitude tests are designed in such a way that very few people ever finish them.

The second type of psychological test which you may encounter looks at *personality and interests*. A typical personality test sets out to measure components such as self-assurance, responsibility, achievement potential, original thinking, values and vocational interests. Interests inventories usually require a person to indicate their level or strength of interest in hobbies, recreation, leisure-time activities and jobs. Personality and interest tests are not usually timed against the clock. Many contain statements or questions to which you are asked to respond by selecting the one that is 'most' or 'least' like you.

When properly used, all such tests provide objective measures against which the interviewer's personal opinions about the candidate, from application forms, previous interviews and so on, can be compared. You will probably benefit from this type of approach, which certainly scores over the rough and ready kinds of interview. But, what really matters is whether the chosen tests measure what they are suppose to measure. In other words, the tests should be related to the job performance required. If you are applying to become a salesperson, for example, questionnaires establishing assertiveness, extroversion and self-reliance may be a good idea. The same dimensions are totally unnecessary for a clerical post.

Should you ask for details about the tests? This is a dilemma: on one hand it may be to your advantage to show 'initiative' by questioning the choice of tests, their fairness and reliability, and how much of the selection decision rests upon them. But you do not want to destroy your chances. You must use your own judgement here, depending on the selection situation and your own personal employment position. You may also want to know about the results – who interprets the tests and to whom the results are made available. Personally, I feel that if an organisation asks you to take a test, you have a right to know the results.

Is it a good idea to practise doing tests? I remember a time when, as a psychology undergraduate (favourite groups for testing tests), I was asked to take a certain personality-type test . . . twice – the first time in Year 1, the second in Year 3. When I compared the scores the main difference, over the years of doing similar tests, was that my 'Lie' score had increased. Apparently I had learned how to fib better! It is possible to buy paperback books about taking tests that may improve your confidence. But, as the majority of tests are only available to qualified users, it is most unlikely you will be able to practise all of them.

Here are some useful tips for first-time testees.

1. Listen to or read the instructions carefully – if you do not understand: *ask*.

2. Make sure you understand which is the reply sheet and how you should mark your answer. Some tests ask you to blacken in ovals, others want you to underline words. Be sure all the instructions are clear before you begin.

3. Do not rush to answer too quickly – but do not take too much time over each question either. Many tests ask for your first reaction. Give it.

4. Test results rarely, if ever, depend on individual answers. Complete as many questions as you can during the time allowed, so your score can be decided upon a number of replies rather than just a few.

5. Some tests are strictly timed, so stop when you are told to stop. With other tests, you can take as long as you like.

6. Don't look for the 'right' answer. Many procedures do not have 'right' or 'good' answers – don't waste time trying to discover where they are.

7. If you feel uneasy about a test or some aspect of the testing situation, there are several steps you can take: you can, of course, refuse to take the test (but note the remarks earlier about asking for test details). Or, you can complete it as requested, but take a careful note of the test name and/or the circumstances surrounding its use. Contact the organisation for an explanation or the British Psychological Society Register of Competence in Occupational Testing (0533 549568) if you remain unsatisfied.

DEALING WITH SALARY

Some employers believe they can engage older workers at low or poor salaries, because any 50 year old will be so 'grateful' for a job that they will accept it at any price. There is a case to be argued for taking a drop in salary in some circumstances: career change is one, but, on the whole, the mature job-seeker should beware of selling him/herself (and the rest of the older population by default) too cheaply.

Most experts agree that it is best to omit any mention of past, present or expected salary in your CV, as it may place you at a disadvantage. At the interview, your prime aim is to secure the job. Do not get involved in pay questions early in the interview or during the first, screening round. Ideally, wait to discuss salary until *after* the position has been offered to you or towards the end of the final interview if it seems to be going well. Stall the discussion if necessary: 'Could we come back to that later when you have told me more about the job?'

Put yourself in a stronger position by having a figure in mind; after redundancy, aim for around 10 per cent more over your previous package. The increase may be in performance-related bonuses, profit-sharing or other creative schemes. An obvious but frequently overlooked tip is to resist an oral offer, however hard it may be. Only accept a salary package when you have an offer in writing.

8

It Wasn't Like That in My Day

THERE IS NOTHING YOU CAN DO about the numbers on your birth certificate, but you can – and must – update your know-how, approach and actions in the modern workplace. You need to familiarise yourself with new terminology and technology. What on earth, for example, was meant by a 'Logistics professional'* in a recent advertisement? You also need to settle in with youthful colleagues, fit in with a less experienced boss, manage an immature workforce and keep an eye open for the next step in your career development.

CURRENT TECHNOLOGY

Computers

Computers are everywhere. You do not have to become an engineering wizard, but you must be familiar with basic operating techniques and standard software operation: word processing, spreadsheets and data bases. Take a course if you have no

---

*Logistics, a term borrowed from the military, is concerned with the integration of many distribution functions in business. It ties together stock control, transport, manufacturing and buying. Modern supermarkets rely on logistics to keep their shelves filled, using bar codes for stock and warehouse information. Training courses at postgraduate level are still evolving.

prior knowledge or experience with computers. Avoid computer programming or systems analysis courses that are for devotee enthusiasts only. Enrol, instead, in training for micro computer operation, keyboard typing, business-application software applications, especially integrated packages such as desktop publishing, ClarisWorks, Microsoft Works.

Many people put off purchasing a computer believing it will be difficult to use, incompatible with workplace systems or quickly out of date. Ask yourself a few key questions first:

- Do I need a system that is compatible with that used at work?

- Do I need to use software compatible with that used at work?

- Do I only need to produce neatly typed documents?

- Do I need to transport my computer?

Here are some answers. There are several personal computer (PC) systems in use. The latest range are based on the Intel 486 processors and are usually called 'IBM compatible'. Older models will not necessarily be compatible with newer systems. If your workplace uses Apple Macintosh, you should purchase an Apple Mac.

You should purchase the same software to use at home as that in use in your office.

For neatly typed documents only, think about a dedicated word processor. These are versatile machines that organise your writing, letters, essays, presentations and other forms of text.

Most PCs do not transport easily, although an Apple Mac is more mobile than most. If you intend to use a computer on the move, consider a portable. Make sure it is not too heavy and that the power life is reasonable. Most have LCD (liquid crystal display) that some older eyes may find less easy to use.

In general, it is best to read PC magazines and consult several dealers before making a purchase. Good stores will let you try before you buy. Ask if there is a 'Helpline' for personal customers, and think about service and spares before you pay bargain basement prices. Enquire about memory size (RAM: the machine's working memory); hard disc capacity (Mb: how much you may be able to store); and integrated software.

Personal organisers

Personal organisers and Apple's Newton are hand-held mini-computers which perform an amazing range of tasks similar to their big brothers. They fit into a handbag, run on regular batteries, are lightweight and connect up to many PCs.

Printers

Printers are necessary to obtain a hard copy from your computer. Dot-matrix prints tiny dots through inked ribbon to form each character. They are excellent value for money, but the results are not as good as new models. Bubblejet and inkjet printers spray ink on to the paper through computer-controlled jets and produce high-quality results. State-of-the-art laser printers offer near perfect reproduction, especially for graphics, at high speed.

Scanners

Scanners capture images from text or pictures, allowing them to be placed on to computer screens. Some accommodate colour, others use grey-scale only.

Modems

Modems are computer attachments connected to information services and other computers.

Fax machines

Facsimile (fax) allows the electronic transmission of paperwork from one user to another. It is widely used, offering instant communication and is fast becoming a standard piece of equipment.

Answerphones

Answerphones are loathed by many, but used by most. Job-seekers should beg, borrow or buy one. They are essential for home office workers. Newer models allow remote access while you are away from home and use just one micro-tape. Create a simple message for incoming callers following the manufacturer's instructions. Avoid saying no one is at home, as it is thought to be an open invitation for unwanted visitors. Make sure the machine is switched to 'answer' or 'on' before you go out.

If you are nervous of talking to an answering machine, here are a few tips.

- Write down what you want to say before calling.

- You are unlikely to run out of tape. You can say a lot in two minutes.

- State your name and where you can be contacted.

- Speak slowly and clearly. Rushing through your message can sound like an asthmatic growl on a tape and will not get your call returned.

- State the day and time of your call.

- Smile while you speak. It lifts up your voice and helps clarity.

Mobile phones

Mobile telephones are a blessing to some, a curse to others. These are the gadgets people keep in their bag or briefcase which give out piercing signals just when you least expect. Use them thoughtfully! Do not have long personal chats when meeting someone else. Instead, develop a fine line in calling people back.

Typewriters

Typewriters these days rarely have to be thumped hard by hand. Manual typewriters have been replaced by electronic machines, with soft-touch and repeater keys, correction tapes (no more whitening fluid!) and memories similar to PCs. Some typewriters are very close to becoming personal computers.

Shorthand remains in use, with *audio* typing commonplace. Small **dictating machines**, powered by small batteries, can be slipped into briefcases and used whenever necessary, without wasting valuable secretarial time. Care should be taken when these are used, however: one lady I know banned her husband from using these machines in their bedroom. It was, she declared 'as if his secretary was in there with them!'

PIN

PIN means personal identification numbers. They are in common use. They are mainly required for obtaining cash from automatic teller machines (ATMs), but their use is expected to grow.

SETTLING IN TO A NEW WORK PLACE

You want to present the best possible image you can to a new employer and new colleagues, so it is important to keep in shape and look trim – but not outdated. No wing collars, sporty blazers, low-cut dresses or beach wear to work, please! At interview, you may have caught a glimpse of the clothes people are wearing. Try to fit in with the style of the office in the early days. Your aim is to become 'one of us' as soon as possible.

You may be surprised at the open plan office arrangements. Office space is very flexible now, able to be rearranged without cost or delay. You will be shown your work area and may have to acclimatise yourself to the ongoing noise and activity close by.

Do not decorate your office walls with photographs of grandchildren at play, military citations or prize pumpkin certificates. While you are justifiably proud of them, they may not appear so interesting to anyone else – and they could date you.

Sexism and racism are old-fashioned and *out*. Watch your

language to and about gender, minorities, other religions. Take care with your own ageist words – by calling others 'youngsters' or similar, you are inviting 'oldie' titles for yourself. It is also important to fix firmly in your mind that crude stories, wandering hands or flirtatious invitations could land you into trouble on harassment charges.

Do not apologise for your age or stage. An older worker returning to work after a gap may worry that everyone will treat him/her as a geriatric or misfit, but this may be needless concern. Bridging the generation gap does not mean appearing in the latest leggings-and-micro-skirt or squeezing that middle-aged belly into over-tight pants. Avoid looking like a frumpy fuddy-duddy and, above all, acting like a know-it-all. If you project just the right amount of confidence without over-brashness or patronage, the chances are that, after a few weeks, your 'age difference' will become invisible.

Younger colleagues

Learning the ropes as a newcomer is a difficult process for everyone, but it can be made smoother by understanding the fitting in process. Natasha Josefowitz and Herman Gadon have written an entire book on the topic: *Fitting In – How to Get a Good Start in Your New Job* (Addison-Wesley). They show how most newcomers of all ages are often excluded from everyday practices at work by those who are on the 'inside'. For example, newcomers may be asked to come into work earlier and stay later than others; they may not get a lunch break or be able to find anyone else to talk to. If the rest of the workforce is very much younger try not to feel as if you have been picked out for special persecution. The most likely explanation is that *all* new-comers are put through a 'fitting-in' process.

Concentrate your attention – learn about your work, your colleagues and your boss. Find out what everyone does and how they do it. Read in-house journals and company notice boards. Keep your eyes and ears open: who knows whom? When and with whom do coffee breaks, lunches and socialising take place? You can help yourself by being pleasant, but not too hearty.

Introduce yourself to everyone, regardless of their response. Show an interest in others, their out-of-work activities, weekends, evenings; attend meetings, interact with other staff as much as possible, and ask for help, advice or knowledge when and where necessary.

It makes sense to stand back for a while from telling your entire life history, family exploits, holiday jokes, work and technical know-how. People will be curious about you – who you are, why you got the job etc., but your main focus of attention and energy should be in getting to know the job. Don't rattle on about domestic matters and avoid making close alliances with colleagues too early. Do not offer details of what you are earning or have earned in the past. Friendly caution seems a good rule to live by at first.

A younger boss

I am finding it a bit tricky getting on with doctors these days. First of all, they call me by my first name, Linda. Although a GP is able to probe and pummel in places nobody else would dare touch, it still seems over-familiar for me to be addressed thus by someone 30 years my junior. And, they keep telling me what to do or rather, what not to do. Is this the way to treat someone old enough to be their mother, I grumble to myself? It's their job, yes, but I still don't like it. They keep comparing me to their parent, too, along the lines of 'My mother is always saying that to me, you are just like her . . .' I bet she doesn't and I'm not.

Having a younger boss can present similar problems – without the physical probing and pummelling, of course! How do you cope with a world of first names, orders from the inexperienced or being treated as if you are someone's parent?

As far as first names are concerned, these days the culture has changed towards the informal, so do not expect any titles or surnames, unless you are at the very highest echelon. Look again at the previous section, and make a point of fitting in with the language and etiquette of your new workplace.

Being treated like a parent instead of a colleague (or patient) is irritating, because it says to me, at least, this person is not

207

really seeing *me*, but a stereotyped person instead. Family roles should not apply in the workplace, but inevitably they spill over from past childhood experiences. You have to decide how to handle this: does the boss do it with everyone or just you? Has your boss ever worked with an older subordinate before? Is he or she really unsure how to handle you? Ask yourself a few questions, too: do you really perceive this young boss as an upstart or harbour resentful feelings about their higher position over your superior experience? A little soul-searching and gentle assertiveness at the right moment may well solve the problem.

Listen intently to your new boss's personal communication style, and try to spot ways of obtaining rapport and trust. There are basically four main normal communication styles, as identified by American psychologist, Dr William Marston. These are active or passive; favourable or antagonistic. Is your boss encouraging, persuasive, outgoing? Or always running late, rude and impatient? Maybe this executive is low-key, lenient, even-tempered, or very precise, orderly and meticulous. Each type requires a different response, one that echoes their own tendencies. Compliment the outgoing types, get to the point quickly with impulsive ones; make friends with the lenient and be accurate with the precise. These are, of course, generalisations, but the main message is clear: use your experience and interpersonal skills to tune in to your superior.

Younger subordinates

If you have inherited a workforce of any age, let alone a very much younger one, you will have different priorities from the start. Natasha Josefowitz and Herman Gadon suggest a group meeting on the first day and 'getting acquainted' appointments with individual staff members later on. Prepare some comments well in advance. Say less rather than more, but ensure your utterances are clear, punchy, professional and friendly. Listen intently to everything said. A useful line in interesting sounding 'grunts' could come in handy: 'Uh-huh?', 'Well, well!', plus encouraging nods and smiles. The image you portray at these early meetings will set the tone for the future, so think carefully about how you wish to be seen. The first days are not the best time to start laying down the law or behaving as a guru on every aspect of the work.

There will probably be a few surprises in store, maybe just a practical joke or two, or something more serious and dramatic. Expect a few shocks to occur and prepare for them. Look back to previous times when you had to deal with the unexpected, and ask yourself how you felt and behaved then. Now use that maturity and experience in your new situation if and when sudden events happen. They are, after all, some of the older worker's key assets!

You are probably well aware that, ideally, personnel or policy changes should be instigated slowly rather than being rushed at with a new 'broom'. But should your brief include cutting back on the workforce or similar trouble-shooting, prepare for the worst. If you have to sack people, it is best to get to the point swiftly and be firm, fair and objective from the start. Of course your employee(s) will be angry and hurt, barely listening to a word you say. But say it you must, accurately and clearly. Do not get caught up in any arguments or personal issues; keep entirely to company and employment policy. Whenever you can, give a person time to digest the news before loading them up with heaps of extra information about pensions, redundancy pay etc.

ARE YOU INDISPENSABLE?

You have found work, you enjoy the job, pay, conditions and colleagues. But, there is a 'something' that niggles at the back of your mind. What can be wrong? Is it the trauma of becoming unemployed all over again and, if so, what can you do to protect yourself? The hints below may help.

Understand, first, that company loyalty is different in the 1990s. Before, when jobs were expected to go on for ever, employees gave their wholehearted commitment to a firm while employers rewarded staff with regular promotion and secure, fatherly protection. Promotion, today, is your responsibility. You must be concerned with and actively promote your own career development. Working hard and waiting may have been successful strategies in the past; today they are no longer reliable.

Recognise which jobs are 'dead-end' or low power and those that can put you on to a more secure pathway. Establish the greater growth areas in your firm and find out which departments are cutting back. Find out different job requirements, whether appointments are generally from within and how applications are handled. Take advantage of performance reviews for career progression guidance and all company-provided training schemes.

Keep a personal file of your achievements and contributions to build up a case for promotion in the organisation. Create a demand for your services by offering effective suggestions. Volunteer for jobs, talk to people at all levels, join in meetings and discussion. Offer your services for a project, if possible as team leader. Learn about office politics. Maintain a sensible, balanced, visible profile: contribute whenever you can, but do not become a nuisance or know-it-all.

Discretion is always a valuable commodity and it is good policy to keep your thoughts about pay and prospects to yourself. You do not want to be perceived as a gossip or gypsy-type worker with a fragmented CV. But, there is nothing to stop you keeping in touch with contacts and networks, especially those who may have helped you towards this point. They need to be contacted and appreciated; perhaps, too, you can do them a favour and gain an edge in your credit. Also, develop some newer friends who have not been used before to help you keep your ears to the business ground.

Robots replace humans, office hierarchies dissolve and administrative staff reduce. American writers presently stress the need for employees to limit their loyalties to sensible levels. Of course, ineffective workers will not be retained, but neither may good performers. You have not bought your job on a freehold, until-death-do-us-part basis. You are a leasehold, rented asset, expendable and disposable. If your company starts pruning the workforce dramatically, take action to protect yourself.

9

Visions of
the Future

RELOCATION

RELOCATION IS OFTEN OFFERED TO EMPLOYEES as part of their career development, but more recently, moving to an unfamiliar area has become the only alternative to redundancy or early retirement. If you are asked to transfer and need to assess the impact on yourself, partner and family, you may find the key points below helpful. They do not, however, cover every aspect of a move. You will need to examine all the details, talk with family members, ask lots of questions and take your time before signing anything.

Companies usually provide good information on financial matters. You should receive written communication about the relocation package well in advance of the move; if it is late or non-existent, request it. Non-financial support should also be available to you. Some companies offer only basic information about the new location and housing to their relocatees. Others include inspection tours and visits, local amenity guides, child/elder-care and education details, counselling, spouse employment assistance, social and community material. Many companies do not write these practical entitlements into their relocation package, but this does not mean that they do not exist. Some say you need to be 'a nuisance' to get all the attention you need, but you should not let this deter you from asking for additional help.

Families are particularly disrupted by relocation. If you have school-age children, working youngsters, an employed partner or dependent relatives, bring them into the decision-making process. Ideally, companies should contact everyone directly, but employers feel this may be an intrusion into your family life. It is up to you to ensure everyone concerned with the transfer is fully informed.

Relocation should never be imposed upon individuals as it leads to resentment, tension and stress. Mutual support and agreement will help keep your relationships strong and your work performance up to the mark. If both partners work, two career moves are involved. Careful pre-planning is necessary here which may need specialist career counselling.

Loss of friends, problems with property, worries about schools and spouse employment may all add up to a gloomy picture. But, given sufficient information and good support, relocation has its benefits too. Recent research by the CBI and Black Horse Relocation Services Ltd indicates that relocation may lead to better locations for bringing up children, moving to a more desirable area and, most important, the prospect of an improved career, promotion and job continuity. For an over 50, relocation may prove an attractive alternative to unemployment.

Some useful books which will be of help if you are considering relocation are: *Relocation – a practical guide*, by Sue Shortland (1990, Institute of Personnel Management) and *Portable Careers – surviving your partner's relocation*, by Linda R. Greenbury (1992, Kogan Page).

MOVING ABROAD

Give me half a chance, and I'm off to the sunshine . . . I think it'll probably be Majorca or Tenerife, had some lovely holidays there years ago. I'll get up slowly, wander down to town, buy an English newspaper, have a coffee,

watch the world go by, do the crossword, have a swim, a
siesta, go out for the evening, have a few beers, do a bit of
work when I feel like it . . . what a life!

Anon, 66 years

Moving abroad has been described as 'a dream that has turned sour for many'. What may seem like an idyllic existence to a holidaymaker can become a nightmare during the winter storms in a tiny uninsulated apartment on the Costa del Sol without anyone to talk to.

If you are thinking about living abroad to take up a job, start a business or retire-plus-freelancing, there are library shelves full of books covering every aspect of the subject. Here, you will find an overview of the most essential points to take into consideration prior to your move.

Where can you go?

Many skilled and qualified people used to emigrate to countries such as Australia, New Zealand and Canada. Not only were these English-speaking areas, but their economies remained strong while others declined. Now these doors are closed to most people. Australian immigration requirements depend nowadays on their own unemployment situation; the Employer Nomination Scheme is for skilled people under 55 years. New Zealand operates an Occupational Priority List, indicating welcome skills; Canada only considers specific skills. South Africa is open to most immigrants. Contact the appropriate authority for current needs.

The USA, while English speaking, has many different cultures, some quite strange to UK immigrants. It is a vast country with great differences between north and south, the Atlantic and Pacific seaboards, and the mid-States. Opportunities do exist, but you will need specialist help to obtain a work visa.

There are few complications to relocating to other Member States of the E.C. These are Belgium, Denmark, France, Germany, Greece, Ireland, Italy, Luxembourg, The Netherlands, Portugal and Spain. The paper barriers are few, if any, but there are other obstacles. Professional qualifications from one country are not always recognised in another. You must check first. Another problem is language ability, for without a good level of fluency, you may be restricted to unskilled work. Consult SEDOC (European System for the International Clearing of Vacancies and Applications for Employment) at your local Job Centre.

In general the following types of work offer better than average opportunities: engineering, computing, teaching, medical (includes nursing), construction and petrochemicals. See also Chapter 4, Gift Work Overseas.

Useful information

Australian High Commission, Australia House, Strand, London WC2B 4LA (also in Manchester and Edinburgh).

Canadian High Commission, MacDonald House, 38 Grosvenor Street, London W1.

New Zealand Embassy, New Zealand House, 80 Haymarket, London SW1Y 4TE.

South African Embassy, Trafalgar Square, London WC2N 5DP.

United States of America Embassy, 24 Grosvenor Square, London W1A 2JB.

What should you take into account before the move?

Apart from sorting out the employment situation, you *must* pre-plan: banking, clothing, cars, children's education (if appropriate), housing (ideally, rent first, buy later), legal matters (especially those related to property inheritance), pensions, visas, work permits, the UK home. These two issues are of prime importance:

Tax and financial planning are absolute essentials. Do not wait until after the move. Start in-depth enquiries and obtain professional advice well in advance of even the most tentative relocation. If you go to live in an EC country, or one with a reciprocal agreement with Britain (Bermuda, Cyprus and Malta are examples), you can receive pension increases. Elsewhere it will be frozen at the rate when you left.

Health and medical matters: Britain has reciprocal health arrangements with other EC countries, but, so it is said, nursing standards, resources and waiting lists are very variable. Ask the Department of Health for EC leaflets. Most other countries do not operate a national health service, so obtain advice on medical insurance. Consult your GP about vaccinations. MASTA (Medical Advisory Services for Travellers Abroad Ltd) is extremely helpful: Bureau of Hygiene and Tropical Diseases, Keppel Street, London WC1E 7HT.

A trial run

It is all too easy to be blinded by the cheap wine and lovely sunshine of a holiday. Instead, practise living in the country of your choice for a minimum of three, preferably six, months *before* making a permanent move. Do not go in high season, stay in a hotel, visit nightclubs or eat in restaurants. Live your life as if you were there for good and within your forecast budget. Visit the bank, church, hairdresser and chiropodist. Try out the medical facilities, find out about the local crime rate, visit the local police station. Get your clothes dry cleaned, do the washing. Rent a TV, car, fridge – and see what happens when it needs repair. Walk to the railway station, take a bus. Is there a library, theatre, cinema, bridge club, casino, race track? If you are used to city life, how will you manage without the bright lights, large supermarkets and high street chain stores? For country dwellers, will you be able to cope with noisy traffic and late night holidaymakers?

Discover how easy/difficult it is to become part of the community, enter into the town's life and make friends – not just fair-weather ones or those who are so desperate for new faces that they will chat to anyone, but people with whom you hope to have something in common. Old friends from home will probably visit you, but they will be far away if things go wrong. Couples should consider what might happen in the future if one of you is left alone or becomes frail. A trial run is a good way of finding out. Think about how you will spend each day in the winter when the shops, restaurants and entertainments are closed, and what remains of the expatriate community battens down the shutters against the winter weather.

Middle stage singles need to think very carefully before moving abroad as they can sometimes be driven – by loneliness and boredom, perhaps – into regrettable or foolish alliances. Single women may find it hard to fit into a world of expatriate couples or may be at the mercy of less than scrupulous adventurers; solo, middle-aged men can expect to be preyed upon by every wily, unattached female for miles around. For both – beware!

Individuals and couples should look at the issues raised in Chapter 4: Gift Work Overseas. Also see Chapter 2: Career Counselling.

Useful books are: *How to Retire Abroad* by Roger Jones and *How to Get a Job Abroad* by Roger Jones (How to Books Ltd).

Saga Holidays, in association with the Pre-Retirement Association, hope to run retirement seminars in Spain for people thinking of retiring there. Contact Saga direct for details: The Saga Building, Middleburg Square, Folkestone, Kent CT20 1AZ.

AND, by the way, there is RAIN IN SPAIN, and FROST IN FLORIDA!

WHAT CAN WE DO NOW FOR THE OVER 50s?

While I have been writing this book, I have noticed an increasing number of press and media articles, programmes and reports highlighting the changes we may expect in both the population balance and the world of work. Here are just a few:

217

Fortune magazine, 8 March 1993, front cover: 'The new unemployed are older and better educated than before, and stand to be on the street a long, long time'. *The Times*, 29 April 1993 report on the Carnegie Trust Enquiry: 'Enquiry calls for rethink on third age'. *The Times Essay*, by Prof. Charles Handy, 3 May 1993: 'A generation rises in search of a role'. *Newsweek*, 14 June 1993, front cover: 'Workers of the world, be warned. The future will have fewer middle-class jobs to offer. Lifetime careers will be rare. Retraining will be constant. Who will win and who will lose?' *The Sunday Times*, 15 August 1993: 'Why catwalk kings are singing the praises of older women'. *Channel 4 Television, Dispatches:* 'The Last Discrimination: What can be done about it?'

While it is encouraging to see these signs, pressure needs to be placed upon many employers to persuade them not to discriminate against older people. Recent research by the University of Sheffield found that 43 per cent of employers consider age to be an important consideration in recruiting, and sizeable numbers of firms still maintain negative and inaccurate stereotypes about older people.

Age discrimination legislation is presently lacking in the UK. There have been various 'guidelines' and 'voluntary plans' organised by the Department of Employment, MPs and government agencies, but, welcome as they are, it is insufficient to deal with what is well described as a 'deep-seated malaise in our society' about older workers.

Corporate personnel policy departments should immediately act upon the Institute of Personnel Management's recent Statement on Age and Employment. In particular, they should take note of this comment.

Employment decisions based on age are never justifiable, are based on fallible suppositions and lead to the ineffective use of human resources.

Organisations should revise their hiring procedures without

delay. To obtain the best available recruits and engage the most appropriate talents to fill their vacancies, they should:

- stop advertising age ranges in job advertisements
- stop asking for age-related data on application forms
- stop using an age bar as a way of pruning job applications
- continue training for all age groups
- train recruitment staff to consider activity-based CVs rather than conventional chronological formats
- train staff about the implications of age discrimination
- consider positive action initiatives to increase the proportion of older workers on their pay roll
- delete the word 'retirement' from their vocabulary
- abolish compulsory retirement, instead offer annual contracts
- offer pre-retirees flexi-time options and/or secondment to voluntary organisations

Other simple initiatives could be taken, many based on the campaigns for women returners. What about over-50 worker role models – not Elizabeth Taylor lookalikes, but real people who, in the middle years, have a success story to tell? Why not offer some special updating and retraining schemes for the over 50s and an over 50 workers' network? What about some enterprising group organising – and sponsoring – a job fair for over 50s?

The word 'retirement' is a damaging one. Contrary to general belief, retirement at 60 or 65 was not handed down with the Ten Commandments. It is a 20th-century concept, started in Europe and put into practice mainly during the 1930s. Now mandatory retirement is illegal in the USA and it is about time we, in the UK, followed our transatlantic cousins by making the concept obsolete. Although the retirement age for women is to be equalised with men at 65 years, phased over a ten year period starting in 2010, this does not go far enough. Retirement should not be enforced on anyone at any age.

Any process of leaving is an important 'rite of passage' and retirement, at any age, should be properly marked with appropriate celebration. John McClean Fox, of Future Perfect, tells of organisations where retirement recognition was so poor that individuals sometimes had to arrange their own leaving parties. Rituals help us make life meaningful: the 'gold watch' is more than a timepiece; it is a symbol of the movement from one role to another. An indifferent attitude to the end of an employee's contribution to an organisation is thoroughly insufficient and damaging to the corporate image. Companies who do not acknowledge retirement should rethink their policy.

Some years ago, Project HAVE Skills, an American programme, set out to help re-entry women with homemaking and volunteer job-relevant skills receive recognition in the workplace. The Project publications included an employer's guide whose opening words are as relevant for work opportunities for the over 50s today as they were to employers in 1981.

> *Most businesses and their personnel executives are interested in finding mature, reliable and experienced workers . . . Yet there is a large pool of just these kinds of people who are under-employed or unemployed.*

> Ruth B. Ekstrom, 1981

By dismissing older people from the workforce, not only do individuals and firms suffer, but so does the whole country. The loss to the UK economy of over-50s' maturity, experience and wisdom is incalculable.

As B&Q plc have found: 'B&Q's over 50s employment scheme has proved that the employment policies of most companies result in, at the very least, a waste of talent. But British industry's loss, it appears, is B&Q's gain.'

GREY POWER – FURTHER RESOURCES

There are, in the UK, around 57 million people, of whom approximately 10,000 retire every week. The population over

State pensionable age is almost 10½ million, while 17 million are 50+ years. The UK 'greys' are fit, healthy and active – and their numbers are growing, with the post-war 'baby-boomers' hovering ever closer to their mid-century birthday. In many industrialised countries, older citizens are fast becoming the majority and, armed with the force of numbers, they are entering the political arena. They tackle and achieve significant gains in key issues such as social security, pensions and ageism. In the USA, political power for the over 50s is well established. The American Association of Retired Persons has over 20 million members, incorporating the powerful political force, the Grey Panthers. Western Australia has the Greypower Party; West Germany has The Greys.

The UK 'greys' are beginning to make an impact, too. When special measures were announced in the November 1993 Budget to assist older persons with VAT on fuel, it was tempting to believe that the strong pre-Budget lobbying efforts of retirees had not been in vain. This was, perhaps, the opening salvo of British Grey Power. If you or those close to you feel that more could be done for the not-so-young, then it is time to let your voice be heard. Here are some of the things you can do:

- write to your MP
- join a retired persons' association
- get involved in local politics
- attend local council meetings
- vote at European, national and local elections
- start up a local campaign
- write to local and national newspapers

Here is a range of organisations with various aims and activities for the over 50s.

Age Concern, 1268 London Road, London SW16 4EJ (age issues, books, free factsheets including No. 19: 'Your State Pension and Carrying on Working'; No. 30: 'Leisure Education'; No. 31: 'Older Workers').

Association of Retired Persons, 3rd floor, Greencoat House, Francis Street, London SW1P 1DZ (age issues, magazine, discounts, local social groups).

Campaign Against Age Discrimination in Employment (Caade), 395 Barlow Road, Altrincham, Cheshire WA14 5HW.

Centre for Policy on Ageing, 25 Ironmonger Row, London EC1V 3QN.

Charity Commissioners, 57 Haymarket, London SW1 0PZ (Central Register of Charities).

City Business Library, 1 Brewers Hall Garden, London EC2 5BX (excellent business reference books, ideal for domestic and international job research).

Equal Opportunities Commission, Overseas House, Quay Street, Manchester M3 3HN.

Federation of Personnel Services, 120 Baker Street, London W1M 2DE (employment agencies).

50-Forward. The Manor House, 46 London Road, Blackwater, Camberley, Surrey GU17 0AA (age issues, travel discounts, magazine).

National Association of Carers, 58 New Road, Chatham, Kent ME4 4QR.

National Council for Carers and their Elderly Dependants, 29 Chilworth Mews, London W2 3RG.

National Council for the Single Woman and her Dependants, 29 Chilworth Mews, London W2 3RG.

National Council of Women, 36 Danbury Street, Islington, London N1 8JU.

New Ways to Work, 347A Upper Street, London N1 0PD.

METRA (Metropolitan Authorities Recruitment Association), PO Box 1540, Homer Road, Solihull, West Midlands B91 3QB.

Relate (formerly National Marriage Guidance Council), Herbert Gray College, Little Church Street, Rugby, Warwickshire CV21 3AP.

Research into Ageing, 49 Queen Victoria Street, London EC4N 4SA.

Women's National Commission, Government Offices, Great George Street, London SW1P 3AQ.

A VISION OF THE FUTURE?

By the time my eldest grandchild – she is presently 11 years of age – reaches 50, the world of work will look very different. Born in 1982 to 'baby-boomer' parents, my granddaughter will reach her majority at the turn of the century. According to current predictions, Jacqueline Louise will stay in education for several years more, perhaps until her late 20s. She will need to be highly trained, with a professional qualification, because, without it, she will not be able to obtain one of the rare 'proper jobs' as we know them today. She will, therefore, start her working life later – and leave it considerably earlier.

Much of my granddaughter's and her contemporaries' lives will be spent in and out of work. They will expect short spells in employment, with career gaps in which to retrain and return to education. They must acquire, early on, excellent career/life planning and development skills. As each job will last less time, so Jacqueline Louise's full-time employment will condense. She will not work as long as her mother and father (or her grand-parents!), although she may work even harder during a short but intensive period. Professor Handy estimates the present-day 100,000 hours of working life will halve to, on average, 50,000 hours or 25 years. 'Work won't stop for such people over 50 but it will not be the same sort of work; it will not be a job as they have known it', he predicts.

This 11 year old can expect to live a very long life, at least into her 90s and probably far beyond. Thoughts of compulsory retirement will not cross her mind. Instead she may never retire or, instead, 'retire' several times. She'll be able to work into her

70s or later, if she so wishes. Most important, she will be part of the majority of the population: older citizens. If all the experts are right (and I suspect they are), within just a few years, organisations will have to acquire more flexible, creative and broad-minded recruitment procedures if they wish to have any staff at all. As young poeple will be in short supply, older workers will be essential.

If and when my granddaughter decides to apply for a job in her middle years, she will not have to worry about all those awkward questions about age or date of birth presently on every application form. Anti-age discrimination legislation will have been passed along the lines of Baroness Phillips's recently rejected House of Lords Employment (Age Limits) Bill. The UK will, belatedly, have caught up with many other countries where negative age discrimination is illegal.

Should Jacqueline Louise become a senior executive or corporate highflyer, she will not have to retire at 60 but she will be able to wait until she is ready. And, even at 70+, she will still be able to serve as a juror (impossible now) and exercise her full rights as a UK citizen. She won't have to keep an eye on her pensions arrangements, either, because flexible earnings will be commonplace.

Most experts agree that by the time Jacqueline Louise reaches her half-century and enters her 'third age', she will be welcomed by prospective employers and have her pick of paid employment opportunities. She will be excited at attaining her half-century because the best years of her life will be yet to come.

For her and the sake of all those whom I hold dear, I hope the prophets are right . . .

Appendices

Appendices

1

Outline CVs

Here is a selection of core CVs. Use them as a guide and adapt them to suit your own circumstances:

1. *Traditional Chronological CV*
2. *Functional Format CV*
3. *Mixed Format CVs:*
    (*a*) *applying for paid work while still in employment,*
    (*b*) *applying for paid work after a short career break,*
    (*c*) *CV after long career break,*
    (*d*) *retiree's CV.*

CV checklist

Have you made sure that your CV

- is one or two pages only?
- is accurate and true?
- uses action verbs?
- omits long descriptions?
- is easy to read?
- is typed or word processed?
- covers 15/20 years only?
- has as few dates as possible?
- starts with your best or most recent experience?
- lists job-related information only?
- includes all your contact details?
- omits irrelevancies?
- uses capitals and underlining?
- states your knowledge?
- states your experience?
- . . . and that it is positive, concise, clear?

1. Traditional Chronological CV

Name
Address

Telephone
Date of Birth
Present Age
Nationality
Status

Education   *Name of school(s), dates attended, full details of GCSE/O and A level subjects taken and results obtained*

Name(s) of further education institution(s), dates attended, full details of course contents and results obtained

Work Experience
Dates   Job Title   Name of Employer   Employer's Address

Interests   *Names of hobbies, activities etc. Example: Art, Music, Reading, Films*

Referees   *Names, position and Addresses*

Optional Extras   *Reason for Leaving*
                            Salary

2. Functional format CV

Name
Address

Telephone

Summary of Work Experience *Generally, a functional CV groups together relevant experience under a number of headings with examples that are related to the skills and experience of the particular job application. No job titles or employers detailed.*

Example:

Budgetary Control *e.g. Committee Work, day-to-day bookkeeping, spreadsheet familiarity, updating and monitoring of investments.*

Skills Acquired *Here list all the skills you have attained and developed. Example: Decision Making*
Teamwork
Time Management

Employment History *Starting with your current or most recent employment, list (with dates) Job Title and Employer. Career gaps may be included here, with brief explanation. Example: Career Break for family responsibilities.*

Key Achievements *This is sometimes included with Employment History to illustrate your contributions to an employer.*

Education and Training *This section lists your qualifications, starting with secondary schooling omitting names of institutions and course details. You may give the dates of recent qualifications. Consider, also, placing qualifications under various headings, such as Vocational, Academic, Post-graduate, Professional.*

Leisure Activities *Highlight voluntary positions of responsibility – or use* **Additional Information:** *other details relevant to the job application.*

3(a). Applying for paid work while still in employment

YOUR FULL NAME
Address

Postcode

Telephone number *(state if Answerphone)*
Fax Number *(only if relevant)*

Present Employment   *(starting date – present)*
Here place details of your specific job title, employer's name and location, your responsibilities, your achievements. Don't waste space with employer's full address; instead, say briefly what the company does, but only if relevant to the job application.

Previously   *Summarise – in reverse order – your work experience over the past 15/20 years only. It is unnecessary to give exact dates as the year is usually enough. If you have had a variety of jobs, group them together – either in 5-year periods or under occupations. Be specific about your job responsibilities and successes – state what you did that made a difference to the employer.*

Education and Qualifications   *State your qualifications and the awarding institution, starting with highest. Avoid giving dates or course details unless obtained within the last 15 years.*

Memberships   *(can include professional associations and/or national, local and community interests when relevant to the application)*

Publications/Presentations   *If any. (NB: Long lists should be on separate page)*

Other relevant information   *This is the place to list any special skills – languages, computing, etc. (Avoid hobbies and interests unless relevant to the job)*

3(b). Applying for paid work after a short career break

YOUR FULL NAME
Address

Postcode

Telephone number *(state if Answerphone)*
Fax Number *(only if relevant)*

Professional Experience *Summarise – in reverse order – your work experience over the past 15–20 years. Give your job title, and describe your responsibilities. State employers' names and location for each job.*

Special Training *Highlight any recent retraining or updating courses here.*

Education and Qualifications *State your qualifications and the awarding institution, starting with highest. Give dates only of courses taken within the last 15 years.*

Voluntary Activities *Show here any team, committee or group work in which you are involved; state any positions of responsibility (Chairperson, Treasurer etc.). Include other unpaid work where relevant to the job.*

Memberships *(may be incorporated with voluntary activities if appropriate – include professional associations and/or national, local and community interests when relevant to the application)*

Other relevant information *This is the place to list any special skills – languages, computing etc. – also military experience if important to the job.*

3(c). Re-entry CV after long career break

Your Full Name
Address

Postcode

Telephone number *(state if Answerphone)*
Fax Number *(only if relevant)*

Your Profile *Insert here a short description of yourself, along the lines suggested in Chapter 1. Keep it short and to the point, without any padding.*

Qualifications *If you have returned to learning during your career break, state date, institution attended, details of the course(s) and achievements. Use the following sub-headings 'Currently; Previously'.*

Work Experience *Including all paid and unpaid/volunteer work in reverse date order. If you have had a career break for domestic responsibilities, then say so but remember to include temporary or occasional activities outside the home. Example: '1982–92: home responsibilities; occasional bookkeeping assignments; treasurer, local PTA; school governor.' Where there is a variety of different jobs over a longer period, you can add one or more of these sub-headings: Other Work Experience; Community Activities; Seasonal Work; Part-time Work.*

Personal Data *Give details and level of proficiency of hobbies and interests, especially those linked to the job application.*

3(d). Retiree's CV

Your Name
Address

Postcode
Telephone
Fax

Availability   *Give an indication of hours, days, weeks, months during which you may be available. For example, if you intend to spend the winter abroad, make it clear you are free from, say, April until October. Omit this section if it is inappropriate.*

Qualifications   *Here state all your qualifications, without dates, starting with the highest.*

Accomplishments   *Indicate what you have achieved during the years in employment – did you gain promotion, live in other countries, acquire a specialist field of knowledge, become a technical expert, build a business? What about your personal qualities – were you always on time, reliable, loyal?*

Professional/Employment History   *List past employers' names, locations. State your job title, dates of employment.*

Membership/Affiliations   *Include professional associations and/or national, local and community interests relevant to post.*

Publications   *Only if appropriate. List separately if necessary.*

2
Bibliography

Anna Alston and Anne Daniel, *The Penguin Careers Guide* (1992, Penguin Books).

Christopher Bainton and Theresa Crowley, *Beyond Redundancy* (1992, Thorsons).

Julie Bayley, *How to Get a Job After 45* 2nd edn (1992, Kogan Page).

Caroline Bird, *Second Careers: New Ways to Work After 50* (1992, Little, Brown and Company).

Klaus Boehm and Jenny Lees-Spalding (eds), *Independent Careers* (1992, Bloomsbury Publishing Company).

E. Patricia Brisner, *Mid-Career Job Hunting – official handbook of the Forty Plus Club* (1991, Prentice-Hall, USA).

Harry Brown, *Retiring Abroad* (1987, Northcote Publishers Ltd).

Rosemary Brown, *The Good Retirement Guide* (1992, Kogan Page).

Careers and Occupational Information Centre (COIC), *Second Chances, National Guide to Adult Education and Training Opportunities*, 1991/2 edn.

Central Bureau for Educational Visits & Exchanges, *Volunteer Work*, 5th edn.

Antony Chapman and Anthony Gale (eds), *Psychology for Careers Counselling* (1982, The British Psychological Society and The Macmillan Press Ltd).

Eldwood N. Chapman, *Comfort Zones: A Practical Guide for Retirement Planning* (1987, Crisp Publications Inc, USA).

J. Robert Connor, *Cracking the Over-50 Job Market* (1992, Penguin Books, USA).

Ken Dychtwald Ph.D and Joe Flower, *Age Wave* (1990, Bantam Books, USA).

Ruth B. Ekstrom, *Project HAVE Skills* (1981, Educational Testing Service, Princeton, New Jersey, USA).

Godfrey Golzen, *The Daily Telegraph Guide to Working Abroad*, 14th edn (1991, Kogan Page).

Linda Greenbury, *Portable Careers* (1992, Kogan Page).

Charles Handy, *The Age of Unreason* (1989, 1991, Random Century Ltd).

Dave J. Hardwick, *Running Your Own Market Stall* (1992, Kogan Page).

Roger Jones, *How to Get a Job Abroad* (1991, How To Books Ltd).

Natasha Josefowitz, *Paths to Power – a woman's guide from first job to top executive* (1980, Addison-Wesley, USA).

Natasha Josefowitz and Herman Gadon, *Fitting In – how to get a good start in your new job* (1988, Addison-Wesley, USA).

Derek Kemp and Fred Kemp, *The Mid-Career Action Guide* (1991, Kogan Page).

Christopher Kirkwood, *Your Services are no Longer Required* (1993, Penguin Books, USA).

Margaret Korving, *The Kogan Page Mature Students Handbook 1991/2* (1991, Kogan Page).

Robert L. Krannich Ph.D and Caryl Rae Krannich Ph.D, *The Best Jobs for the 1990s and into the 21st Century* (1993, Impact Publications, USA).

Kenneth Lysons, *Earning Money in Retirement* (1992, Age Concern, England).

Nella J. Marcus, *Fifty Plus* (1991, Macdonald Optima).

Munton, Forster, Altman and Greenbury, *Job Relocation – managing people on the move* (1992, John Wiley & Sons).

Albert Myers, *Blueprint for Success – the complete guide to starting a business after 50* (1991, Newcastle Publishing Co, USA).

Robert Nathan and Michael Syrett, *How to Survive Unemployment* (1981, 1983, Penguin Books).

Dave Patten, *The Daily Telegraph Guide – Successful Marketing for the Small Business* 2nd edn (1992, Kogan Page).

Joan Perkin, *It's Never Too Late* (1984, Impact Books).

Amin Rajan, *1990s: Where Will the New Jobs Be?* (1992, The Institute of Careers Guidance and the Centre for Research in Employment and Technology in Europe).

Susan Ratcliff, *How to Be a Weekend Entrepreneur* (1991, Marketing Methods Press, USA).

Samuel N. Ray, *Résumés for the Over-50 Job Hunter* (1992, John Wiley & Sons, USA).

Maggie Smith, *Changing Course* (1989, 1992, Mercury Books).

Nancy Tuft, *An Active Retirement* (1992, Age Concern, England).

The Women Returners' Network, *Returning to Work 1991/2* (Kogan Page).

3
Useful Addresses

The following addresses are given **in addition** to those already included in relevant chapters.

Age Concern, 1268 London Road, London SW16 4EJ.

Association of Retired Persons (ARP), 3rd floor, Greencoat House, Francis Street, London SW1P 1DZ.

British Association for Counselling, 1 Regent Place, Rugby, Warwickshire CV21 2PJ

British Psychological Society (BPS), St Andrews House, 48 Princess Road East, Leicester LE1 7DR.

BPS Register of Competence in Occupational Testing – RCOT – Telephone: 0533 549568.

Careers and Occupational Information Centre (COIC): *Orders for books, leaflets*: PO Box 348, Bristol BS99 7FE. *Enquiries*: Moorfoot, Sheffield, South Yorks S1 4PQ (*Scotland*) 247 St John's Road, Corstophine, Edinburgh EH12 7XD.

Central Bureau for Educational Visits and Exchanges, Seymour Mews House, Seymour Mews, London W1H 9PE.

Institute of Careers Guidance, 27a Lower High Street, Stourbridge, West Midlands DY8 1TA.

Institute of Personnel Management, 35 Camp Road, London SW19 4UX.

Occupational Pensions Advisory Service, 11 Belgrave Road, London SW1V 1RB.

Oxford Psychologists Press Ltd, Lambourne House, 311–21 Banbury Road, Oxford OX2 7JH.

Royal College of Needlework, Apartment 12a, Hampton Court Palace, East Molesey, Surrey.

Index

wives, 35–7
women:
  education, 149–50
  self-employment, 143–4
  wives, 35–7
Women Returners Network, 13
Women's National Commission, 223
woodwork, 108
word processors, 202

work content skills, 48–9, 152
Work Portfolio, 10–11
work 'shadowing', 61–2
Workers' Educational Association, 154
writing, 117

younger bosses, 207–8
younger colleagues, 206–7
younger subordinates, 208–9